PROCLAIM THE WORD

SUNDAY HOMILIES
YEAR A

THE
SEASONAL SUNDAYS
AND
MAJOR FEAST DAYS

First published in Great Britain in 1991 by
KEVIN MAYHEW LTD
Rattlesden
Bury St Edmunds
Suffolk IP30 0SZ

ISBN 0 86209 208 6

Typesetting and page creation by Anne Hallam
Printed in Great Britain by J. B. Offset Printers (Marks Tey) Limited

CONTENTS

ABOUT THE CONTRIBUTORS

Sybil Boddington SND   is a Notre Dame Sister, currently engaged in spiritual formation.

Aelred Burrows OSB   is Lecturer in Scripture and Church History at Ampleforth Abbey.

Lavinia Byrne IBVM   is Associate Secretary for the Community of Women and Men in the Church at the Council of Churches for Britain and Ireland.

J. D. Crichton   is known internationally as a liturgical scholar, and is author of *The Coming of the Lord* and *Journey through Lent*.

Daniel Cronin   is Chancellor of the Archdiocese of Westminster.

Patrick Crowley   is parish priest of St Winifred's, Heaton Mersey, Stockport.

Eamon Duffy   is a Fellow of Magdalene College, Cambridge and a University Lecturer in Theology.

Philip Egan   is the Assistant Catholic Chaplain to the University of Cambridge.

Margaret Hebblethwaite   is author of *Motherhood and God* and *Finding God in All Things*.

Kevin T. Kelly   is Lecturer in Christian Ethics at Heythrop College, University of London.

Kieran Kettleton   works for the Catholic Fund for Overseas Development in London.

David Konstant   is the Bishop of Leeds.

Janet Lash   is a teacher, parent, and member of the East Anglian Diocesan Adult Religious Education Commission.

Monica Lawlor   is a retired university teacher who now works as a clinical psychologist in a hospital for people with learning difficulties.

Bill Mason   served as an Anglican priest from 1954-1987, subsequently becoming a Catholic.

Phelim McGowan SJ	is a priest of the parish of The Sacred Heart, Wimbledon.
Michael McMahon	is an assistant priest at St Mirin's Cathedral, Paisley, and a Lecturer in the New Testament.
Jim McManus CSSR	is Provincial Superior of the Redemptorists in Britain.
Anthony Meredith SJ	is a member of Campion Hall, Oxford.
Brian Newns	is parish priest of St John Fisher, Widnes.
Anthony Nye SJ	is Spritual Director at Allen Hall Seminary.
Joseph O'Hanlon	is Lecturer in New Testament Studies at the Franciscan Study Centre, Canterbury.
Tony Philpot	is parish priest of Our Lady and the English Martyrs, Cambridge.
Terence Phipps	is Precentor of Westminster Cathedral.
H. J. Richards	is a songwriter and author of many popular books, including *Focus on the Bible*.
Arthur Roche	is parish priest of St Wilfrid's, Leeds.
Anthony Shryane	is parish priest of Our Lady of the Annunciation, King's Lynn.
Anthony E. Sketch	is parish priest of Our Lady, Star of the Sea, Lowestoft.
Aelred Smith CP	is Rector of the Passionist Retreat House at Minsteracres, County Durham.
Austin Smith CP	is a member of the Passionist Fathers' Inner City Mission in Liverpool.
Colin Stewart	is Co-ordinator of the Ogilvie Centre for Religious Education in the Diocese of Aberdeen.
David Watson	is Chaplain to the University of Hull and Humberside Polytechnic.
Peter Wilkinson	is parish priest of St Clare's, Liverpool, and is well known as the author of the *Focus on the Sacraments series*.
Richard Wilson	is a priest of the Diocese of East Anglia.

PREFACE

T O THE 'regular' seasonal Sundays containing Lectionary readings that change from year to year are added, in this volume, Mary, Mother of God, the Annunciation, The Transfiguration, The Triumph of the Cross and All Souls. This will ensure that *Proclaim the Word* will cover, as well as the Sundays, all the Feasts on which a sermon might well be given, or to which the preacher would wish to refer on the preceding or following Sunday: these are the punctuation points of the Church's year. The outline homilies contained in this book were not written to be preached *verbatim*, although many of them would stand that test: each is one individual's response to the challenge given in the liturgy. The stimulus they will give to the reader may not be one of agreement, but if they provoke any response, they will have served their purpose.

It is not only preacher or group leader who stands to benefit from this book. Many, Catholics and others, have found in *Proclaim the Word* a unique programme of weekly reading and an aid to private prayer and meditation, based on the Lectionary.

FIRST SUNDAY OF ADVENT

Isaiah 2: 1-5; psalm 121
Romans 13:11-14; Matthew 24:37- 44

Preparing for Birth

T ODAY IS the first day of the liturgical year. More than that, it is the first day of a three-year liturgical cycle, because it is the First Sunday of Advent in Year A. So it is truly a time for making a fresh start.

Advent, as we all know, is a period of preparation for Christmas. It is a sort of pregnancy time, when we look ahead and get ready for the new birth. In any pregnancy there is excitement that our lives are going to be changed in such a marvellous way. But there may also be some apprehension. We are going to have to make some changes in the way we organise our lives, rearranging our time and our finances. We should pay special attention to our health and fitness, turn up to our antenatal classes and check-ups, and maybe read a book that prepares us for the course of labour. As the birth approaches we have to be ready at any moment to get into the car and go to hospital, with the house in order and our bag packed and the crib made ready for the new baby.

So too with Advent: we have to make sure we are ready. 'Stay awake,' says Jesus, 'because you do not know the day when your master is coming... stand ready because the Son of Man is coming at an hour you do not expect.' The original context for this gospel, and for the epistle by St Paul, was the expectation of the Second Coming. But in the Advent liturgy we apply these sayings to our celebration of the First Coming, at Christmas. And even though we know the day in advance – we know Christmas Day is 25 December – there is a deeper point that remains true. God can surprise us by coming at any time, and we should be ready.

There is a sense in which this readiness for the unexpected coming of the Lord is good, traditional Catholic stuff. Some of the older people in the congregation may have been brought up on the principles of the Penny Catechism, which urges us to go to sleep in a spirit of readiness in case we die in the night: 'After my night prayers I should ... occupy myself with the thoughts of death; and endeavour to compose myself to rest at the foot of the cross, and give my last thoughts to my crucified Saviour.' Catholic theology has always been rather good at planning for the unforeseen emergency. Suppose a baby was born sick and might not live till its christening? Then a baptism can be carried out by a layperson, pouring water on the baby and saying 'I baptise you in the name of the Father and of the Son and of the Holy Spirit.' Suppose someone was on her way to being baptised in church when a bus knocked her down? Then she would receive the grace of baptism by desire. The Church, as our spiritual mother, is well prepared for accidents, rather like the mother who instructed her daughter never to wear tatty underwear because you never knew when you might be unexpectedly knocked down by a bus.

But joking apart, Advent is a serious time of preparation, not just for ordering the turkey, getting out the decorations and buying the presents, but for preparing our hearts for the coming of Jesus. Just as in any pregnancy, we need to reassess and maybe rearrange our time and our finances, in the light of the gospel call to share. From next week the Advent texts turn to John the Baptist, who came to prepare the way of the Lord by teaching us, 'If anyone has two tunics they must share with the one who has none, and the one with something to eat must do the same' (Lk 3:11). Our equivalent of antenatal classes and check-ups might be attending an Advent prayer group, or receiving the Sacrament of Reconciliation. In place of a book on labour we might choose some spiritual reading. To attend to our spiritual health, we need to set some time aside for prayer. One spiritual director used to say we should spend at least a quarter of an hour in prayer every day because, he said, 'then you will always be ready'. Ready for what? For death, maybe, but more often for the daily demands on our love that call for a ready generosity.

St Paul calls on us in the epistle, to 'wake up now'. 'No drunken orgies, no promiscuity', he says. We might feel that did not apply to us, and stop listening, but the next words have a message for everyone: 'no wrangling or jealousy.' There is a way in which each one of us can make ourselves more ready for Jesus, whether it is by setting aside our disputes or jealousies, by devoting a little more time to prayer or spiritual reading, or by working out a just proportion of our income to set aside for the needs of the poor. These are all ways in which we can take Advent seriously and say with happy anticipation, 'Come Lord Jesus'.

Margaret Hebblethwaite

SECOND SUNDAY OF ADVENT

Isaiah 11:1-10; psalm 71
Romans 15:4-6; Matthew 3:1-12

The Story of Salvation

WHEN we were children most of us loved fairy stories. They transported us into a world where the impossible happened, and where there was nothing strange in children being wiser, stronger and more successful than adults. They were mythical stories about the never-ending struggle between good and evil. They were often frightening stories, but deliberately so, so that we might learn by imagiation how to master even the worst hardships and difficulties. Although these stories were an escape from the real world into one of fantasy, their hidden value was an education in hope through which we slowly began to discover that good in the end does triumph.

Isaiah speaks of hope in words that are redolent of such stories. The wolf lies down with the lamb; the cow and the bear are friends; children play with poisonous snakes and are unhurt. It is a time of idyllic peace when all contradictions are resolved and fear has disappeared from the world. In those days good will finally have overcome evil. But this is no fairy story; it is the story of our salvation. What Isaiah speaks of is a genuine hope in the coming of our Saviour, who would be filled with the Spirit of the Lord. He would take on his shoulders the whole weight of the world's evil and sin. He would have all the gifts we associate with God's Spirit: wisdom, insight, counsel, strength, knowledge, reverence and fear of the Lord. He would be the man of complete and utter integrity, someone whose faithfulness will be like the faithfulness and loyalty of God himself. He would be called Jesus, the Saviour.

The people of John the Baptist's day were thirsty for hope. Life was hard and it was difficult to recognise God in the midst of it all. If in God's days (as the psalmist says) 'justice shall flourish and peace, till the moon fails', then how could these times be God's times? Was it not more likely that these were days of a famine of the word of God, marked by his absence and indeed by his anger? There was great injustice; there was much poverty. The Jews lived under a harsh colonial power; they felt the pain of slavery. They were uneasy about the future. And of course they suffered the common ills of the poor everywhere – malnutrition, homelessness, unemployment, sickness, early death.

This was the world that the strange man John, known as the Baptist, was familiar with. He was a breath of fresh air, as fresh as the air of the desert he came from. He was untainted by the evils of society and was a symbol of hope. People flocked to him. They listened to him, they confessed their sins to him, and they were baptised as a sign of their repentance. His message was starkly simple: 'Repent, for the kingdom of God is close at hand.' It was a message of confident hope that was immediately appealing to his hearers.

One of the remarkable things about the people who were baptised by John is the way they listened. Their belief in God had a kind of wholeness about it; they believed not just with their heads but with their whole being, so their faith affected all they did. It was simple and direct faith. In spite of all the hardships they saw God in their daily lives and acted accordingly.

Each age has its own faults. Perhaps one of our common feelings today is our slowness to recognise God; even believers can be sluggards when it comes to this. Advent is a time to try to recapture some of the simple faith of our forebears: a time to look for God more attentively, to recognise him more readily, and to live according to his word more closely. St Richard of Chichester's prayer says 'I pray that I may know thee more clearly, follow thee more nearly and love thee more dearly.' In trying to do this we can do no better than follow John the Baptist's advice: 'Repent ... Confess your sins'. Truth doesn't change; what was good and necessary for the people of John's days is good and necessary for us today. There is a wholesomeness, simplicity and directness in John's advice that can only be good.

If I confess my sins I will come to know myself better and discover more of my needs, my weaknesses and my poverty. Then I shall be better able to declare myself to God, to believe and especially to hope. His Holy Spirit with all the gifts he brings (gifts without number – not just the seven mentioned by Isaiah) will be with me and will teach me how to grow more and more into a person of integrity, so that I may be true to myself, to my neighbour and to God. Then indeed I shall be ready to welcome the One of complete integrity, who saves me, carries my burdens and makes me whole – Jesus, the Saviour.

This is no fairy story, but the account of our salvation.

David Konstant

THIRD SUNDAY OF ADVENT

Isaiah 35: 1-6,10; psalm 145
James 5:7-10; Matthew 11:2-11

Taking Stock

WHO AMONG you, having been awarded a fresh job, has undergone a training course? That is, some preparation for your work, a getting ready for fresh understanding, renewed application of yourself to your responsibilies. Or indeed, who has gone off for in-service training, while working 'at post'? You have time set apart for appraisal, the learning of new skills, to develop progress. Many services use this general facility; tractor-drivers, teachers, social workers, trainees of all sorts are sent off to identify fresh perceptions of their occupations.

This idea of time out for training is not confined to the world of work. Christians in retreat do the same thing: taking time, often away from home, to consider themselves, God's purposes for them, and how best to obey.

The liturgical season of Advent is similar. Our mother Church asks us now to take stock, consider and think out our response to God who, through Mary, has come among us as the Christ.

Four weekly strides are set out, in the path to Christmas, in the readings for the Advent Sundays. We began two weeks ago, by asking God to stir up our wills (as the Book of Common Prayer robustly translates the ancient collect) We should be doing good, in order to greet Christ with a proper welcome when his perennial birthday comes. On the Second Sunday of Advent, the Church moves us on to ask for individual sorrow for sin, which hinders our sight of God. From that note of penance we look forward now, on the Third Sunday, with great happiness, to the great birthday ahead on December 25th. And beyond that we look onwards and upwards to Christ's second arrival. The question meanwhile, for us today is: how can we experience the joy of salvation which the collect for today, asks for? I ask you now to think about how today's readings can help you. I ask you to think about how the 'last things' of christian doctrine can be real for us. It is rather frightening! Can we even now know something of death, judgement, heaven and hell? Knowing the last things, or about them, is called *eschatology:* a useful summing up word. The last things have often been seen as vehicles of dread. Let us see them as vehicles of joy (at least, the first three).

Part of the joy of the christian life is the happiness of knowing that Christ has come. I can say that Christ and his works have arrived. How?

By hearing his message to St John Baptist in the gospel for today, which I ask you to glance at. John, in Herod's awful prison, was desperate for an answer. He managed to get a message to Jesus: 'are you the one, or do we still wait?' the Lord effectively tells St John to wait no longer. He, Christ, is the fulfiller of prophecy. Isaiah, whose words we hear today forecasting the kingdom, had been justified. That kingdom, replied Jesus to the Baptist, is now being inaugurated, and even the most humble and ordinary church member is somehow greater than John, in the light of this kingdom.

Can you therefore see yourselves in that light? Because it is very important indeed for understanding what a Catholic Christian is. In Baptism your status is assured; you are 'in Christ'. You are working out this status with all its privileges and responsibilities. You look forward to even greater glory when all is fulfilled. So this Third Sunday of Advent is the time to allow yourself that spiritual induction course, the in-service training, with which we began. Pray that you become *what* you are, become *better* than you are, and that in God's time you will become *perfectly* what you are.

Now we live in the kingdom and anticipate its fullness, by serving Christ in his kingdom. Today's portion of Isaiah the prophet shows the world how. In Isaiah's verses, written on the verge of national collapse and the threat of takeover by the current super-power, we see a pattern of relief work of an interesting range. I believe that the kingdom has arrived on earth, because of the many charities, all around us. Be they Red Cross or Red Crescent, the aid agencies show the motives and effects of the kingdom: it is so interesting to hear Isaiah, so unfortunately brought up to date. If we want to realise our life in the kingdom, here is a ready help to hand – in helping to relieve those in desperation. Be encouraged, realise fulfilment if you are already motivated into working for and helping the poor. So many are.

The Third Sunday of Advent is the Sunday of anticipation; we anticipate the kingdom in its glory by aiding its growth now; by helping the Lord of today's first psalm verse to get justice for the oppressed ones, bread for the empty-bellied, release from the world's terror-gaols.

St James, in second reading, spices our recipe of spiritual good today. As you strive, he tells us, do all with patience, tolerance and courage. May your coming Christmas be all the happier for today's message from the Word of God.

Bill Mason

FOURTH SUNDAY OF ADVENT

Isaiah 7:10-14 psalm 23
Romans 1:1-7; Matthew 1:18-24

Son of David, Son of God

O N THIS the last Sunday before Christmas the readings seek to prepare us to celebrate the feast of Christ's birth. In particular they show us how Jesus is *Son of David* and, what is much more, *Son of God.*

Today's Gospel has been called the 'Annunciation to Joseph' and indeed it concentrates on Joseph's reaction to the pregnancy of Mary, who would be his wife once he had taken her from her parents' home to his own. The angel's message makes clear to Joseph 'that Mary has conceived what is in her through the 'Holy Spirit'. Joseph is to name Mary's son Jesus, a name which means God saves', because he is to save his people from their sins. Matthew sees all this as fulfilling Isaiah's prophecy which we have as our first reading today, about the son of a virgin who will be called *Emmanuel* a name which means 'God-is-with-us'. All of this leads us to conclude that Jesus is indeed the Son of God.

But we also need to realise that this Gospel comes immediately after the genealogy of 'Jesus Christ, Son of David, son of Abraham', with which Matthew begins his Gospel. That genealogy ends with 'Joseph, the husband of Mary: of her was born Jesus who is called Christ'. When the angel appears to Joseph he addresses him as 'Joseph son of David' – this shows us the part Joseph has to play in the birth of Jesus. Through Mary and the Holy Spirit, Jesus is the Son of God. Because he is accepted and named by Joseph, because Joseph becomes Jesus's legal though not physical father, Jesus can truly be called Son of David.

Son of David has been called the most Jewish of all Jesus's titles. Despite the failure of David's line in political terms the people, supported by the words of the prophets, placed their hope in the coming of a son of David who would deliver them, and in 70 AD and as late as 90 AD the Roman Emperors Vespasian and Domitian were seeking descendants of David to kill, lest they should serve as a focus for popular unrest.

Furthermore, *Son of David* leads to *Son of God.* Through the prophet Nathan God promised to David that he would be a father to David's offspring and successors on the throne and that they would be God's sons. At their coronation they were adopted by God as his sons, and became his representatives to the people. According to Matthew therefore, because of Joseph and Mary, and of course the Holy Spirit,

Jesus is both son of David and son of God. But clearly he is son of God in quite a different way to all other descendants of David.

In today's second reading, the beginning to St Paul's Letter to the Romans, we are told about the 'Son of God, who, according to the human nature he took, was a descendant of David but who in order of the spirit, the spirit of holiness that was in him, was proclaimed Son of God in all his power through his resurrection from the dead'. Here the insufficiency of the title *Son of David* is apparent, since it is contrasted unfavourably with the proclamation of Jesus as *Son of God* through his resurrection.

This text seems to reflect an early stage of Christian thinking which saw Jesus revealed as God's Son through his resurrection. Later, in St Mark's gospel, we find this revelation of Jesus as the Son of God at his baptism. Then St Luke and St Matthew show Jesus to us as Son of God at his conception, while St John reveals him as the pre-existent Son of God from before creation.

Our first reading from the prophet Isaiah, takes us back to the *Emmanuel* prophecy, which Matthew sees as fulfilled by the birth of Christ. The original prophecy is likely to have referred to the imminent birth of a son and heir to Ahaz. The Davidic dynasty, threatened as it is by attack from Syria and Israel, will therefore survive, probably in the person of Ahaz's son Hezekiah, one of the few good kings of Judah. It refers neither to a virgin birth nor to the Messiah, at any rate when taken literally.

The Greek version of the Old Testament, the Septuagint, translated the Hebrew word *alma*, young woman, with *parthenos* a virgin. So now Matthew has at his disposal an Old Testament prophecy which speaks of a virgin conceiying and giving birth to a son, a prophecy addressed to the 'House of David', that is a descendant of David, and the child is to be called *Emmanuel*, meaning 'God-is-with us'. Given that he is trying to explain how Jesus is the son of God, born of the Virgin Mary, and yet descended from David through Joseph's legal paternity, he saw the Isaian prophecy as a godsend, and who are we to say that he was wrong?

These texts therefore invite us to preach yet again, and perhaps at greater length than is possible on Christmas Day, not merely the Christmas *story* but the Christmas *gospel*. The baby born to Mary and named by Joseph is truly God and truly man, son of God and son of David. The limitations of the latter title are evident but it has its importance, linking Christ's life with God's preparation for his coming in the Old Testament. And it demonstrates for us the significance of St Joseph, something often forgotten or minimised.

Brian Newns

CHRISTMAS: MASS AT MIDNIGHT

Isaiah 9:1-7; psalm 95
Titus 2:11-14; Luke 2:1-14

A Simple Sign

C HRISTMAS is such a familiar feast, centred on children and returning us to our childhood. It is a feast of family, God made Man at home with humanity. There is a feeling of homeliness about the crib, the carols, the depiction of the scene in so many works of art.

It could become just a celebration of nostalgia, of easy good will and good cheer, a value sentiment of kindliness towards our neighbour . Simply a pleasant 'at home' with this world's goods, the commercial Christmas. We need to go back and read the gospel account again, to hear what it is really saying. What do we find? That it is not just talking about being at home on this earth and about natural human values, important though they may be at one level. The circumstances of this child's birth are not what we would expect, however accessible and near to us their family setting may be. There is a tremendous poverty about them, a radical humility and trust in what is asked of Mary and Joseph. Poverty, humility, trust – these are a special emphasis throughout St Luke's gospel. They begin already in the Saviour's birth, a pattern which will be traced out in the whole of Jesus' life, leading to the poverty and humility of the cross.

The birth takes place at such an inconvenient time, a time of upheaval throughout the Roman Empire, and in this small corner occupied by Roman troops and controlled by an alien governor. The upheaval is caused by a census for tax purposes. In the ancient world a census entailed not simply returning a form but physical presence, uprooting oneself from work and home to go to one's place of origin. The gospel account puts it simply and unemotionally, starting with the head of the household. 'Joseph set out from the town of Nazareth in Galilee and travelled up to Judaea, to the town of David, since he was of David's house and line, in order to be registered'. It proceeds, saying much in little, 'together with Mary, his betrothed, who was with child'. The previous chapter, in the account of the Annunciation to Mary by the angel Gabriel, had told us the special nature and role of this child: Son of God and Saviour, whose birth would come through the overshadowing of the Holy Spirit, not through any man's seed. All through the high providence and power of God, recalled to us by the first two readings of this mass: a light to those who have walked in darkness, bringing a peace that has no end, making salvation possible by

God's grace for the whole human race. How strange and unexpected then that God in his providence should plan the birth in this way. Mary having to travel during her pregnancy, Joseph having to care for her in such trying circumstances, and all because of an ukase from the Emperor Augustus in distant Rome. The narrative goes on with an equal simplicity and economy of words: 'While they were there the time came for her to have her child, and she gave birth to a son, her first-born, and laid him in a manger because there was no room for them at the inn.' That is all that is said about the poverty in which the Son of God becomes one with the lowest of the low, the outcast, the refugee, the travelling people, the homeless. It is accepted by Mary and Joseph, and the evangelist, with total humility and without fuss. Blessed be God, it seems to say, for this is the way he has visited his people and redeemed them. It simply happened that way because there were so many other people who had come to Bethlehem to be registered. No privileges, no going to the head of the queue.

Everything presents a challenge through ordinariness, which questions our lives. What really matters? Wealth? Comfort? Convenience? Honour? None of these things that the world of consumerism and power politics esteems. Simply doing God's will, following God's plan, whatever it costs. Mary and Joseph teach us this. So does the Christ child in his silence and utter dependence. 'And here is a sign for you; you will find a baby wrapped in swaddling clothes and lying in a manger'; a deep and clear sign given to the shepherds because of its humility, sheer poverty, self-emptying. Shepherds, those unexpected first visitors; not kings, not priests, not scholars; but ordinary working men keeping watch over their flocks out in the fields by night. The angel's appearance, and the glory of the Lord shining round them, filled them with terror by its utter strangeness. Had not even Moses approached the Lord with fear and dread? Yet the angel spoke to them of peace, joy, salvation, and gave them a sign very close to their own occupation. They would find the child laid in an animal's feeding trough. They received that message and that sign with simple trust, like Mary and Joseph, and came immediately to Bethlehem. May we journey there in spirit tonight to receive the message trustingly into our own lives.

Anthony Nye

16

CHRISTMAS: DAYTIME MASS

Isaiah 52:7-10; psalm 97
Hebrews 1:1-6; John 1:1-18

The Word of God

WHAT a lyrical, poetic opening to today's liturgy, on a morning which for most of us still holds the magic and enthralment of childhood memories of this lovely feast!

Isaiah's words of exultation are applied to the great news of Christmas, the news that the Messiah has finally come, bringing good news, heralding peace, bringing happiness and proclaiming salvation. He seems to compare the days of waiting in Advent with watchmen who have remained at their posts, eagerly awaiting the arrival of their Lord, and shouting for joy when he comes. There's also a lovely picture of God 'baring his holy arm', throwing back his cloak as if to move into strong action to save his people.

The responsorial psalm moves us immediately into a hymn of thanksgiving and praise. We are invited to sing, shout, ring out our joy, and sing with harp, the sound of music, trumpets and horn. And all the earth is encouraged to join in, because we 'have seen the salvation of our God.'

After all that enthusiasm, we have a gentler, more reflective announcement from the author of the epistle to the Hebrews. He writes of how the prophets spoke of the coming of the Messiah, and of how in our time God spoke through His Son. In his own quiet way the author uses powerful words to describe the Son sent by God: 'He is the radiant light of God's glory and the perfect copy of his nature...he is far above the angels.'

As we turn to the gospel we are once more into the realm of poetry, with the sublimity of John's words: 'In the beginning was the Word.' *logos* was the word used by John: the visible, tangible Word of life, mentioned by him in his first epistle. The word *logos* has several meanings: the power to bring into being, the empowerment to *be*. So the application to Our Lord of the term 'word' has great significance. Even in our own language 'word' has powerful connotations: it can be 'a signal for action', a 'promise', an 'utterance', 'taking someone at their word'. All imply a strength and a power. The Word of God uttered by the Father is a person, the Son of God.

John's words move steadily on in an attempt to convey the *logos* as always being in existence, as distinct from the Father, yet being God himself.

17

In the beginning was the Word:
the Word was with God;
the Word was God.

The word *logos* is also interchangeable with the word 'wisdom'. St Paul called Christ the 'Wisdom of God' in 1 Corinthians 1: 24. It is equivalent also to supernatural life and light as John continues: 'All that came to be had life in him, and that life was the light of men.' And later, speaking of the mission of John the Baptist he says, 'He came as a witness, as a witness, to speak for the light ... He was not the light, only a witness to speak for the light ...The Word was the true light that enlightens all men.'

'Word' is used in the psalms with the same aspect of power: 'God created the heavens by his Word .. By the word of Yahweh the heavens were made and of the earth it is written: "He spoke and it was created"' (Ps 33).

In the book of Genesis, Chapter 2, the power of the word used in naming the animals is given to Adam. God brought to Adam 'all the wild beasts and all the birds of heaven ... to see what he would call them; each one was to bear the name the man would give it.' Adam's ability to name, to use a particular word for each animal had its own power. Although this is allegorical we accept the inner meaning of what is expressed in figurative language: namely the power implied in naming. Compare the receiving of our names in baptism, when we become Christians, individually called to follow Christ.

It might be illuminating and helpful to see what use we make of words. Coming from us they can be either life-giving or utterly destructive.

Sometimes even refraining from using words can be damning and harmful. How often do we refrain from praise when we see people making efforts to please? How often do we fail to say 'Thank you' for services done, no matter how small they are? Whereas if we spoke words of affirmation, we could bring real joy into people's lives. Using words of praise, kindness, appreciation, encouragement can make all the difference in the world to those who receive them. As Browning said in another context: 'the little more and how much it is!' And we hear of 'damning with faint praise.' How wise our poets were in their knowledge of human nature!

Finally St John says: 'The Word was made flesh, he lived among us.' Let us pray that our words may bring life not death to all who hear them.

Sybil Boddington

THE HOLY FAMILY

Ecclesiasticus 3: 2-6, 12-14; psalm 127
Colossians 3:12-21; Matthew 2:13-15, 19-23

Mine to Love

'**J**ESUS was good, and obedient, and always did what Mary and Joseph said at once, without arguing.' At the age of eight, I regarded Sister Véronique's statement with a jaundiced eye. Because she made the Holy Family so boring; and because, clearly, she was making it all up. It didn't say that in the gospel, not word for word, anyway. It was just a way of blackmailing her class into behaving. The secular arm was shanghaiing us with religious weapons. By using Nazareth as a piece of disciplinary equipment, she made it wimpish, distasteful. And so it remained, for me, for years. Only as an adult did I come to appreciate the beauty of the Holy Family at Nazareth.

Nazareth was the place where the Son of Man was brought up. Jesus is God's way of being human. He is the peak, the summit of humanity. And here, at Nazareth, humanly, he was formed. Here the character grew, strong, straight and slender – not warped and distorted, not wounded or lopsided. Here he was prepared for unpopularity, disappointment, betrayal, torture and death. Here he learned affection, toughness and tenderness, self-confidence and dignity; here he learned to use words sublimely. This character was not formed amid the razamatazz of tutors, colleges, regiments, but in a monumental stillness, in a one-roomed hut in a marginal village in a forgotten province, by a pair of inconspicuous peasants called Mary and Joseph. They passed their philosophy of life on to Jesus, without ever realising how wise and good they both were. The process was quite unselfconscious.

We think of the formation of our own children, and appreciate the miracle. What struggles we have! Struggles to stop our sons and daughters being materialists, to make them unselfish, to stop them being jealous of other children, to stop them being worldly-wise before their time, to make them calm and not nervous and fractious, to give them an instinct of prayer, a habit of prayer. As a humble priestly observer, watching from the sidelines, I have huge sympathy for parents. I know it really isn't easy. How can we avoid passing on our agenda, our prejudices, our hang-ups, our blind spots? We try our hardest. But we don't always succeed.

The beauty of the Holy Family was in the 'being' and not in the 'doing'. The gospels tell us little about it. It is as if the evangelists had drawn a curtain in front of those thirty years, so that Our Lord could get on with being himself, undisturbed. His life must have been simple, the routine colossally regular. Nazareth was his universe, his cousins and neighbours peopled his world. The faithful observance of the religious calendar, the learning of a trade and the earning of a basic living – simple, slow, deliberate, deeply human things. They left time for observing human nature, watching the seasons and the crops, finding the hand of God in the texture of daily life, the contemplative dimension of life, ruminating, wondering at the Father's greatness, experiencing his love. We cannot slavishly imitate the Holy Family (because we live in the 20th century, not the first; and because we have insufficient data, anyway) but can we try to incorporate this reflective quietness into our domestic scene?

The logic of St Paul to the Colossians, today, is this: your awareness of being loved by God should be so keen that it remodels your behaviour. The normal thing is to be argumentative, tart, short-tempered, not to suffer fools gladly. But once the wave of God's affection has swept over you, your dealings with others – including the intimate members of your family will be infected by your experience. You, following God's pattern, will be gentle.

It's the argument which underlies our marriage teaching. If a Christian is what she or he is meant to be, how could she or he *not* bring an awareness of God's faithfulness into marriage? How could a really Christian bride or bridegroom take any other pattern for enduring love than that of Christ? If 'Now I live, not I, but Christ lives in me' is true at all, doesn't it have to be true in the way I live my marriage?

Somebody once said that every handbook of moral theology should have a final chapter entitled, 'In practice, however .. '. We have ruefully to admit that most of us Christians – including Catholics – are not consumed by gratitude towards, and love of, God. That while the biology of marriage is something we have known from a very early age, the chemistry of it (reactions of two people under one roof) has proved a different matter altogether. And that often our family relationships may have more of a pagan base than a religious one. The fidelity between husband and wife may be modelled on how the neighbours behave, not on any divine indwelling. The affection between parents and children may be cooled by all kinds of things, things which are basically quite selfish.

Today's reading from Ecclesiasticus lays a clammy hand on the modern heart. As a priest I can think of old people who live in homes, warm, dry, fed, but unvisited by children who live a few miles away. One must always allow for the exceptional case. Some parents make themselves unvisitable! But in other instances, you feel, the children have mentally put their old parents in kennels. They don't grudge the cost ('After all, one has a duty....we're not savages, I'm glad to say'), but the one gift withheld is the gift of inclusion, in the lives of the second and third generation. The unspoken message is 'We will do our social duty by you, but actually, you've become irrelevant.' Ecclesiasticus's programme is different: we are to 'respect', we are to 'honour', we are to 'set at ease', we are to 'show sympathy'. The rift which occurs horizontally, between generations, in our culture, is almost as scandalous as the vertical rift of divorce. We are called to be a countersign to all this; to draw on our spiritual resources to make our family life radically other than that of the sealed-off, precarious nuclear family.

One of the wickedest things done by industrial countries at the time of the slave trade was to discourage marriage and divide families. You can see the result centuries later. A country like Nigeria or Kenya still has family bonds intact, and the instinct to care for the extended family is still healthy and strong. But in Sierra Leone, the land of freed slaves, those instincts have been killed, and you find street-children cast adrift. Have we turned into a sophisticated, manicured Sierra Leone?

We need to remind ourselves, all of us, that our blood relations are the ones God has given to us, above all others, to cherish and to care for. If we had planned things we might have equipped ourselves with a different family altogether, a less irritating, more agreeable one. But God did the planning. And his plan was that this concrete set of people, with these characteristics, should be given to me; in his providence, they're mine to love. What kind of a hand do I make of it?

Once a year, the Church reminds us of the ideal. What you're like, she says, governs the way you relate.

Tony Philpot

MARY, MOTHER OF GOD (JAN 1)

Numbers 6:22-27; psalm 66
Galatians 4:4-7; Luke 2:16-21

Mary, the Woman of Prayer

MANY of us find it difficult to see the relevance of Mary in our lives today. Perhaps it's because when we were brought up our sinfulness was emphasised and Mary was portrayed as the only light in a dark and sinful world. The hymn 'O purest of creatures' characterises it perfectly. We were taught to see ourselves as the naughty child, brought shame-faced to his mother whom he had hurt, rather than a good child being drawn to his loving mother. Furthermore, there was a gulf between the Christian and the world in which he lived, a world full of temptation. He was to set his eyes on the world to come, rather than to contemplate the world around him.

To give a Marian dimension to our spirituality today, we might find it helpful to try and see what the Father hopes to accomplish in each one of us, rather than concentrating on what he has accomplished in Mary. Mary is the model, 'the exemplar of faith and charity' as Vatican 2 puts it, the 'Woman of Faith' as she was called by the Fathers of the Church. But, today, we could also see her as 'Mary, the Woman of Prayer', as each of us is called to be a prayerful person, even, maybe particularly, if we are leading a busy and full life.

It is significant that it is while she is at prayer at the time of the Annunciation (Lk 1:28), that Mary, by the power of the Holy Spirit, receives the Son of God firstly into her heart and then into her body. By her *fiat*, by her unquestioning faith and openness to the Spirit, she becomes the Mother of God before she becomes the physical mother of Jesus His Son. As the second reading, puts it, 'God has sent the Spirit of his Son into our hearts: the Spirit that cries out, "Abba, Father!" and it is this that makes you a son. You are not a slave any more.' It is from the fruit of her prayer that Mary bears Jesus into the world. The immediate outcome of Mary's meeting with God in prayer was her meeting with Elizabeth; she went, Luke tells us, 'as quickly as she could' to her cousin. Like Mary, we are asked to bring Jesus into our lives, and then bring Jesus into the world. What she did in her unique way we can do in ours.

Prayer involves a double journey. Firstly, we travel inwards and open ourselves to God, penetrating – and assimilating – the mind of Jesus (Ph 2:5), and then we return to the world, and face the everyday issues of life, but with a new sensitivity to the Father's will in all things, attuned to the mind and heart of Jesus. The closer we get to God in prayer, the greater the love we take to others in our daily lives.

We can see this two-way process in the first reading, where Moses passes on God's blessing to Aaron and his sons. Moses, God's friend, was already blessed and, like Mary had 'won God's favour' (Lk 1:3g). If he had kept this blessing to himself, he would have rendered it powerless and ineffective. Only when it is passed on to others, does it reach fulfilment. Moses, by handing on this blessing to his people, gives glory to God and at the same time, allows God's will to be accomplished in him.

The contemplative dimension of Mary is clearly seen in the gospel chosen for today's feast (Lk 2: 16-21). At Bethlehem, she reflects on the shepherds' message, 'as for Mary, she treasured all these things and pondered them in her heart.' This is Mary's response to the words of both the angels and of the shepherds. She is just as astonished as everyone else at what the shepherds have to say. 'Everyone who heard it was astonished' but only Mary is reported to have reflected on the events, interpreting them in her heart.

The shepherds had listened to the voice of the angel and so they, in their particular way, were able to bring Jesus to Mary and Joseph. Mary, the contemplative, ponders the Word of God coming from her fellow human beings as well as from God. Her pondering on all that has been said is mentioned four times in St Luke's gospel and, it would appear to be her habitual response to mystery. Yet, in the midst of her reflection, Mary is, quite literally, holding the object of her contemplation, Jesus, the Son of God!

The shepherds make the connection between 'what they had seen and heard' and return to their flocks glorifying and praising God, who accomplished such great things, as Mary said in her *Magnificat*. The shepherds are perhaps the forerunners of all believers, who will glorify God for what they have heard and praise him for what they have seen.

We will see the relevance of Mary in our lives today, if we try to emulate her in prayer. Many of us hear the Word of God at mass and various liturgies but do not always spend time treasuring that word so that it becomes part of us.

If we begin to ponder the Word of God, by using it as a source for our prayer, maybe, we will, like Mary, begin to understand the mind and heart of God and be able to bring his Son Jesus to birth in our lives and in today's world.

Phelim McGowan

SECOND SUNDAY OF CHRISTMAS

Ecclesiasticus 24:1-2, 8-12; psalm 147
Ephesians 1:3-6, 15-18; John 1:1-8

The First Blessing

G EOFFREY Chaucer, 'the first finder of our language', obliquely attests to the sublimity of the opening verses of John's gospel in his portrait of the wanton and merry friar:

> *For thogh a widwe hadde noght a sho,*
> *So plesaunt was his 'in principio',*
> *Yet wolde he have a ferthing, er he wente.*

The majestic overture had become a blessing formula, a prayer whose efficacy was sought to right an illness or ward off an evil. Newly baptised children were blessed with John's words and, indeed, amulets containing them were worn for protection against misfortune. The old Latin missal preserved the mediaeval estimation of the grandeur of the Prologue by insisting that it be read at every mass. The Last Gospel, as it was known, was part of the final blessing. In our own time, it provides the gospel reading for no less than three masses of Christmastide.

The reason for the prominence of John's Prologue may lie in its fulness. It is as perfect a statement of God's way with the world as could be. The great resevoir of Israel's words, the Old Testament, is called upon to serve the poet who hymns this canticle of the Son. The words, the images, the metaphors, the very rhythms of its poetry are harnessed to new and daring thoughts.

'In the beginning ...' The opening words of the Book of Genesis are pushed beyond time. From eternity it was God's intention to be with us, to speak to us. For the Word was always with God, waiting to be uttered. Indeed, the Word was God; the very being of God is to be open to humanity, eternally to be ready to speak, to utter us into being.

'And God saw everything that he had made ...' Everything is from God, is of the Word. Everything speaks of God, of the Word. In the work the craftsman is recognised. For the very life of humanity comes from God: 'he breathed into his nostrils the breath of life and man became a living being'. Beyond that giving, yet inextricably bound to it, is the Word's giving of eternal life: 'I am the living bread which came down from heaven; whoever eats of this bread will live forever and the bread that I will give for the life of the world is my flesh' (Jn 6:51). The

Word becomes flesh in order that the flesh of humanity may hear the Word and believe and 'have life in his name' (Jn 20:31).

The eagle-soaring of John's opening verses must not propel us into the realms of fantasy. The coming of the Word is to be rooted in a time and place, among a people. The witness (a very important word in the vocabulary of this gospel) is, indeed, sent from God but openly declares, 'I am not the Messiah' (Jn 1: 20). John's ministry is to point to the 'Lamb of God who takes away the sin of the world' (Jn 1: 29), indeed, to bear witness that 'this is the Son of God' (Jn 1: 34).

The true light through whom creation came to be, came into the Baptist's world, the world of humanity. The capacity to believe, to come to the light, is, by divine gift, a human possibility: 'and his disciples believed in him' (Jn 2: 11). But there is another possibility: 'people loved darkness rather than light, because their deeds were evil' (Jn 3: 19). For the light of the world not only enlightens, it exposes.

As the body of the gospel will tragically reveal, 'his own people did not accept him'. We need to be cautious here. The Prologue and the rest of John's story presents the Jewish people as universally hostile to Jesus. But this cannot have been so. The earliest Christians were Jews such as Andrew, Simon Peter, Philip and Nathanial and the whole first generation of Christians. The fourth gospel reflects more the animosities of the end of the first century rather than the enthusiasm with which Jesus was received when he first walked the hills of Galilee.

In the beginning the Word was. Now the Word is becoming. In the beginning the Word was with God. Now the Word is with us. In the the beginning the Word was God. Now the Word is flesh. The surprise is not in the Word's becoming flesh; rather, it is in the bold insistence that the presence of God is in the thick of humanity.

The presence 'lived among us'. More evocatively, 'pitched his tent amongst us'. For the allusion is to the divine injunction to the Exodus people to pitch a tent, a tabernacle, to be a dwelling for the Lord, the focus of his presence, among them (Ex 25: 89). The prophets looked to the day when the divine dwelling would be permanent: 'I will dwell in the midst of the people of Israel forever' (Ezek 43: 7). The temporary tent is replaced by the humanity of the Son. The *shekinah*, the glorious divine presence pitched in the heart of the people, is there for all to see.

The presence does not come amongst us as a threat. It is full of graciousness, of loving-kindness. That is what grace and truth imply. The poet is pointing to that covenant of love which joins the heart of God with the hearts of his people. The 'Son, who is nearest to the Father's heart', turns his father into our father.

Joseph O'Hanlon

EPIPHANY

Isaiah 60:1-6; psalm 71
Ephesians 3:2-3a, 5-6; Matthew 2:1-12

Star of Truth Within the Heart

A STAR for the child. A cross for the child become the man. Both set in the gospel story to blaze as beacons for all the nations. They are placed at the edges of redemption like lamps set either side of a door to guide and welcome all inside. The light of both encircles that tableau of christian hope: a mother and her son.

The star in scripture heralds a kingly figure so the search began in the corridors of kingship and power. But the only help there came from the Word of God and not from the king. Those with earthly powers only do not understand power except in terms of rivalry, competition, dark deceptions, and false pledges of homage. The word of the world-wise can hide hidden agendas and mislead the unwary. Revelation is from God and its proof is a shining word which leads faithfully to the truth and brings exceeding great joy.

But the quest for truth is not easy. The dangers of deception and dead-ends are real. Its discovering is a matter of life and death. Truth leads to unfathomable riches, undiminished joy, a sense of rightness, that life can be trusted as good. Deceit delivers nothing. It diminishes, shrinks, withers love. Trust is not at ease and is gradually withdrawn. Movement ceases, the quest ends.

But the true word moves us onwards, curious to find our future. Truth does not try to keep us tied. It trusts itself and its power to find an echo in every sincere heart. It allows the seeker to go in freedom confident in its own inner light to find the God from whom it comes. It does not need the support of sages or kings. Not even God is needed to underwrite truth. It is of him and knows itself to be in touch with all reality. It knows that it will lead whoever follows its path to places of peace and to a trust which cannot be disputed or doubted. Truth shines with a wisdom that gives lustre to life.

An evangelist asks only that the reader follow their own inner wisdom, their own light and intuition for what is right. Truth and goodness are to be found in christ, child and man. People will know it if they but come to him with a sincere mind and a trusting heart. Whether they meet Christ as a silent child in the arms of his mother or as the quiet man in the lap of the grief-stricken Mary truth will recognise truth. At the sign of the star or the place of the cross the wisdom of God's love will make its appeal and seek a verdict in adoration.

This is the vision of the prophet Isaiah. Though darkness floods the sky above the cross, or night mantles the mother and her child in Bethlehem, nations and kings would come to those hills of new dawns. It will not be a seeking for the brash brilliance of passing glory. That is transient, and inadequate to satisfy the human search for lasting value. The coming will be to the glory of the divine hidden within the corners of human hearts and homes. The attractive tableau is of a nurturing love and spacious trust: a welcome place at last for all to end their search.

Because of that trust gifts can be confidently uncovered and laid before life for safe keeping and use. They will not go unrecognised or be treated with indifference. Each single gift would be touched and acknowledged. Life's touch of acceptance would enrich the gift as diamonds sparkle with fire from the light which falls on them. All our gifts and giving can be unfolded in the presence of this child and this man. None will ever be ignored and none scorned. All will be welcomed with the delight and gratitude of their royal recipient.

This Epiphany is a time of light. The light that falls around this feast and this head is star-light, hearth-light, lovelight. Those who come near to it can take it away with them. It can be cupped in the hands and a heart of faith as one cups a candlelight against the night. It can be carried into other homes, other hearts, other far countries. We can all take this grace with us.

As we do older lights, other glories of man-made kings, politics of power, illusions of spendour will begin to pall in the stronger and firmer light of truth. Fashions that fail to sustain will fade, as colours are drained by the sun. Truth lived in love is a light which will never dim or be quenched. It never sinks, sets or ceases to shine. This star of truth within the human heart living by love is always there even when threatened by the darkness of evil. The child followed his star to a crown of thorns. His next Epiphany was in no hidden corner but in a public place. All would again be drawn to that crowning glory. And all again would pay homage to a God of infinite love.

Aelred Smith

THE BAPTISM OF THE LORD

Isaiah 42:1-4, 6-7; psalm 28
Acts 10:34-38; Matthew 3:13-17

The Beginnings of Ministry

O NCE we have celebrated Christmas, it is rather difficult to get worked up about anything else too quickly. The Feast of the Epiphany seems to come far too soon, and since we have already sung *We Three Kings* and other such carols at Christmas their effect is rather lost when January 6th appears. In fact, the Western Church has always rather downplayed the Epiphany and this has led to a lack of understanding of its true significance.

This has never been the case in the Orthodox Church. There, the Epiphany was far more important than Christmas, since the Epiphany celebrated the more dynamic aspects of the Incarnation – when Christ actually showed himself to the whole world. For Eastern Christians the Epiphany had three parts: the coming of the Magi, the Baptism of the Lord and the wedding feast at Cana, since at all these moments Christ manifested or showed himself to the world as Son of God. These elements, it is true, were also in the Western feast of the Epiphany but it is only in recent years that we have given Christ's baptism a special focus and made it a separate feast on the first Sunday of Ordinary Time.

So why is the baptism so important? Certainly, it has been something that people have found difficult to understand over the years, and the first person who found it difficult was John the Baptist himself. Poor John exclaims: 'It is I who need baptism from you and yet you come to me!' He has been preaching repentance and has actually managed to get a number of Jews to undergo baptism (a practice normally reserved for converts to Judaism) and now here is the man he knows to be the Messiah coming to submit to his baptism. The one who is totally sinless comes to receive a baptism that takes away sins. The one who takes away the sins of the world seems to convict himself of sin by his humble ritual submission.

But perhaps there is some sense in it all. Jesus has been waiting to declare himself, and John by his extraordinary preaching has convinced the people of their sinfulness and their need of the Messiah who is about to appear. Jesus, by undergoing baptism, legitimises and makes sense of the ministry of John and in the scenes that accompany it gives us the meaning of his own ministry. In these few verses in Matthew, Jesus is baptised, receives the Spirit (almost like Confirmation) and is picked out – or 'ordained' – as God's chosen Son. His ministry has begun spectacularly and now he has to live out the calling he has so publicly been given. John's work is over. His baptism of repentance now makes way for Christ's baptism, which brings with it the whole of the Paschal Mystery.

The words used by the voice from heaven 'This is my Son, the Beloved; my favour rests on him' take us straight back to the passage from Isaiah we read for the first reading. This is one of the so-called 'songs of the Suffering Servant' and we can see that Jesus is quite deliberately cast in this role. Today the emphasis is on his ministry: his bringing of true justice, his serving of the cause of right, opening the eyes of the blind and freeing captives. But we cannot read any of the songs of the Suffering Servant without remembering that his call was to suffering and death, and therefore we cannot understand the ministry of Christ without realising the importance of the cross and resurrection. Just as the shadow of the cross and the glory of the resurrection hang round the crib at Christmas, so this momentous manifestation of Christ's sonship is shot through with images of his suffering, death and final glory.

A further question we might ask is 'Who is this manifestation for?' After all, John's baptism was a peculiarly Jewish affair, an attempt to convince the chosen people of their wrongdoing. With the beginning of Christ's ministry we see a quite different thrust. His adoption of the role of the Suffering Servant makes him a 'covenant of the people and light of the nations' (the *Lumen Gentium* of the Vatican II Decree on the Church) and in the second reading we see the consequences of this gradually dawning on the early disciples: 'The truth that I have now come to realise,' Peter said, 'is that God does not have any favourites.' Jesus Christ is Lord of all people and his ministry had to extend beyond the Jewish nation and reach the ends of the earth. We who have been baptised with Christ are the fulfilment of that ministry and are heirs with him of the great promises of God. In a very real sense we share in Christ's work and to us too are addressed the words of the Father 'This is my Son, the Beloved; my favour rests on him.' If we accept Christ as Redeemer and Lord and share with him that favour of God, then we too have work to do and suffering to endure. It may not always be pleasant but it will be worth it, for one day – please God – another voice will resound from heaven and say to us 'Come, you blessed of my Father; enter the kingdom prepared for you from the beginning of time.'

Terence Phipps

THE ANNUNCIATION (MARCH 25)

Isaiah 7:10-14; psalm 39
Hebrews 10:4-10; Luke 1:26-38

The Word Takes Flesh

H AVING a baby is a very physical thing. The whole process, from conception through pregnancy to birth and beyond, is about bodies – about men's bodies and women's bodies, about sperm and ova; about breasts and wombs, blood, amniotic fluid, milk and colostrum.

Christian piety often shies away from thinking physically about Jesus's coming, as if the earthly reality might somehow conflict with the credal statement that here, uniquely, God's self-revelation is so complete that we have to say of this child that he is God himself. Today's readings, at first blush, seem to give credibility to this piously non-physical view. There is no whiff of sex or passion in this conception; instead we have Isaiah's sign of a virgin. Mary has only to say *fiat*, 'Yes, so be it' in answer to angelic soliciting, and the child is conceived. To modern ears this seems a rejection of the physical: we are offered a child without sex, fruit without seed, the spiritual without the material.

If we are to understand the readings, however, we have to hear them as the early Christians, and their Jewish forebears, would have heard them. We have, in order to do this, to wash our ears of the distortions of much that has passed as Christian piety. We have to rid ourselves of the idea that 'spiritual' means thin and ghostly, floating free of irritating bodily limitations to some ethereal world outside the world we know. We have to kill the notion that virginity matters because it is physical wholeness, unspoilt by the messy confusions of sex and childbirth. We have to abandon the suspicion that confessing Jesus as Lord entails believing him some not-quite-human kind of Superman.

Of course the physical matters when a baby is conceived, but not the 'merely' physical. Only if something seems to be going wrong will a couple expecting a child start thinking about hormone levels or placenta function. In the normal way they'll be concentrating on more exciting things: on names, or how to decorate the nursery; on what kind of pram to buy, or on imagining a glorious future for their offspring. They will be thinking in short, about a person not a body.

A friend of mine, after hearing that her baby daughter would never walk, said her first thought was, 'Now she'll never win Wimbledon!' I believe that was a genuinely spiritual response. What she was crying out against, as mother, was the cruel curtailment of the infinite possibility she dreamed of for her child. Walking, she saw, is not a value in itself;

walking matters because of what it enables us to do. Similarly, the sign of virginity points us beyond the merely physical. It speaks of our incapacity and God's power. It says we are as incapable of gracing our world into godliness as a virgin is to conceive. It asserts that only by God's own action is he with us, *Emmanuel.*

And yet, today's readings tell us, God's power is not coercive. We have to *accept* the offered gift. We have to be virginally *open* to God's action. Mary is truly the Christ-bearer not because she bore him in her flesh but because she opened her heart to him in faith. 'You do not ask for sacrifice and offerings but an open ear,' says the psalmist. In our ordinary lives we are well aware that being parents means much more than physical procreation. Except in the most drearily physical sense, giving birth does not establish the relationship between mother and child. Adoptive parents can 'really' be mothers and fathers; natural parents may not really be parents at all.

Mary was Christ's mother in faith before she was mother in the flesh. Faith established the reality of her motherhood. Because she responded in humble openness to God's free invitation, she proclaims in her flesh humanity's most faithful response to God's action in our fleshly world. Amazingly, God can only utter his Word in our world if we open ourselves attentively to him.

Today's second reading, from the letter to the Hebrews, brings together all these elements. It is about rejection of the crudeness of mere flesh, about acknowledgement of our powerlessness to redeem our world, about the saving incarnation of God in Jesus. 'Bulls' blood and goats' blood are useless for taking away sins,' the author declares. Instead we have Christ, in flesh: 'Sacrifices and offerings thou hast not desired, but a body hast thou prepared for me.' His body, like the body of every child born into the world, bears within itself the inescapable certainty of death. In accepting his death ('Then I said, Lo, I have come to do thy will O God!') he makes a spiritual offering of his flesh in obedience to God's will. 'And by that will we have been sanctified through the offering of the body of Jesus Christ once for all.'

In the Annunciation the mystery is entire. In the enfleshment of God in the flesh of our common humanity the possibility of human wholeness becomes actual. The paradox of fruitful virginity leads us to the paradox of the cross. By entering our world, God committed himself to death for our life. By opening herself to God's enfleshment, Mary became the sign and first-fruit of mankind's redemption from its tragic entrapment in mere flesh. In bringing forth the Saviour she became the first of those who are saved.

Janet Lash

31

ASH WEDNESDAY

Joel 2:12-18; psalm 50
2 Corinthians 5:20-6: 2; Matthew 6:1-6, 16-18

Personal Holiness

THE CROWDS of people seen streaming out of any city centre Catholic church on Ash Wednesday are a most compelling act of witness to the faith. It is one of the few occasions when we can proclaim to the world non-verbally that we are Christians. The mark of the ashes made on our foreheads is there for all to see.

Again it is a day when everyone in the community admits that they are 'living in sin' in one way or another and are in need of repentance. Therefore, unlike the reception of the Eucharist, there is no reason why every single person in the church should not take part in this communal penitential act. Even the prophets of the Old Testament could hardly have made it easier for us. They hold out a marvellous incentive and encouragement for all of us to take that essential step: 'turn to the Lord your God again, for he is all tenderness and compassion, slow to anger, rich in graciousness and ready to relent.'

St Paul is very conscious of the dignity which belongs to each baptised person and goes on to use the apt analogy of being an ambassador for Christ. An ambassador represents his country which means that he has to be close to the Head of State who sends him; they really need to be of one mind. So with us and the God whom we are privileged to represent; it makes no sense whatsoever to be at enmity with him. As ambassadors we have to be reconciled and now is always the acceptable time, with Lent being the perfect opportunity to make our apologies for our sins. It is a time for entrusting the past to the mercy of God, to be freed from the burden of guilt, so that we may do our best in the present and the future.

The Ash Wednesday liturgy contains a call to personal holiness which should spill over into works of mercy, particularly almsgiving and 'willing service to our neighbour' (Preface). It is interesting to note St Matthew's insistence on doing all these things with great sensitivity and discretion. More often than not, when we speak of almsgiving, we usually intend it for the materially poor. St Vincent de Paul was very fond of reminding his companions that the poor are 'our lords and masters', and that one day we will have to be forgiven by them, depending on how we gave our alms. If we give grudgingly and make others feel very small by our manner of giving then there is much that is deficient about our charity.

When the Church encourages us to fast today and on Good Friday, she is trying to point out the importance of discipline in our spiritual lives. Once we become too accustome to self-indulgence, then so many things can go by the board, and we become spiritually flabby. Sadly human nature being what it is, even the act of fasting can be abused; it can all too easily degenerate into a parade of outward show. If we do things just to impress others and win their admiration, then our motives are bound to be less than pure – we may do many impressive things, certainly, but for all the wrong reasons.

That even has to be said about our prayer life sometimes, especially at public prayer. It is not always the outwardly pious ones who are closest to God. Rather we are invited to 'be still and know God', which can often happen best in the privacy of our own rooms, where our relationship with the Lord can deepen and develop. In this setting we have the possibility of being briefed for that honoured role as an ambassador for Christ. Then we are ready to go out to do our part in building up the kingdom of God in our world.

So Lent is an opportunity, given to us by the Church to use well in making our inner selves grow strong, and to do so discreetly. Three times in today's gospel these words are emphasised: 'and your Father who sees all that is done in secret will reward you'. It is never easy to find time to spend with God, but this great tradition of the Church provides us with a marvellous incentive to make that effort.

Daniel Cronin

FIRST SUNDAY OF LENT

Genesis 2:7-9, 3:1-7; psalm 50
Romans 5:12-19; Matthew 4:1-11

Lead us not into Temptation

S ED LIBERA *nos a malo!* This final petition from the Lord's Prayer is the one least considered by the twentieth century and yet surely the most pertinent. For despite man's remarkable, nay spectacular progress in many sectors, on another level this last century with its global wars, unrighteous structures and manifold deprivations must rank (especially in the West) amongst the most inhumane. As G.K. Chesterton once observed, original sin is the most obvious thing in the world (cf Second Reading). Never before have we been so aware of the psychological, social, economic and even ecological devastation sin causes – the tree of knowledge (First Reading) – and yet never before have we been so unwilling to face up to the challenge it presents. The next millenium must needs be built afresh. This is why today on, the first Sunday of Lent, the call to repentance, 'Bring us back to you' (alternative Opening Prayer) has a truly prophetic resonance.

But let's be radical. For it is no use bemoaning the plight of the world's poor – crying 'Have mercy on us, O Lord, for we have sinned' (Responsorial Psalm) – unless I personally am willing to change: after all, my sins and excess are partly to blame. We speak so glibly of freedom, but little of the responsibility that must go with it. The first task of our Lenten pilgrimage with Christ, the second Adam, is *ressourcement*, 'going back to the basics'. This is why the Holy Spirit has led us into the desert, for it is in the desert that we are brought face to face with the facts of life and the facts of death (Preface of Lent II).

For Israel, as for the Fathers of the Church, the desert was where the spirits of evil lurked, the place where Christ met – neither for the last time, nor for the first – Satan (Gospel). Of course, to speak of the devil and his minions is unfashionable nowadays, outmoded; but, truth to tell, without an adequate demonology some areas of human experience – for example, the odd atmosphere, suicide and despair, habits of sin difficult to break – become inaccessible (cf Rite of Communion). On the other hand, the desert was also the *locus* of divine liberation, where God worked signs and wonders, notably the water from the rock and the manna that fell from heaven. We need the annual 'desert-experience' of Lent, as an earnest of renewal. After all, who have I become, and where am I going? What is the most important person or purpose or thing in my life? Is my relationship with God advancing or stagnating?

Indeed, only in this radical perspective can I acknowledge my sins – they have impaired or wrecked my intimacy with the Lord, crucified my loving Saviour Jesus Christ, and worst of all offended God's infinite goodness, Act of Contrition – and invoke the help I need to do something about them (Preface of 1st Sunday of Lent).

For *Deo gratias!* one man in human history really did take on the devil – on his own terms – and emerge victorious; furthermore, he has promised us the victory if we act through him, with him and in him (Second Reading). This is the doctrine – in relation to the wood of the cross – of today's gospel, Christ's inaugural retreat. Having been baptised at the Jordan, confirmed with the Spirit and declared by the Father to be the Son of God, we now see him in the desert as the Son of Man, fully human, like us in all things but sin (Eucharistic Prayer IV). Moreover, it is on Christ's very humanity that the devil plays with his three temptations to lust, pride and power. After all, Christ was hungry, and how wrong would have been a quick miracle of convenience? And since God was looking after him, could he not try it out, just for once? Besides, surely there was an easier way of being Messiah?

The Perfect Human Being, however, has given us a different 'Philosophy of Life' as the key to human happiness and fulfillment. This is the philosophy of *Fiat voluntas tua,* 'Thy will be done on earth as it is in heaven', total obedience to God's will, the Way of the Cross. For conversion is precisely God's gift: an ongoing, indeed life-long process, affecting heart, mind and action (Preface of Lent III). We must on our part be prepared to change, to suffer and to die, to be tempted, tried and tested (although, as St Ambrose taught, never beyond our ability and never without being given the necessary graces).

Which is why the lenten journey is not primarily about what I do for God, about self-denial or doing something extra: Tradition would in any case recommend not one, but three lenten works of prayer, fasting and almsgiving! Rather – and this is not to counterfeit our cooperation with grace nor the vestments of purple – the lenten Liturgy is all about what God does for us. In fact this is a season of joy, a special gift, the favourable time when God brings the image of his Son to perfection within us (Preface of Lent I). At the dawn of a new millenium, Lent should therefore bring a ray of hope, grounds for confidence, a reason for celebration. After all, in Old English 'lencten' means Spring.

Philip Egan

SECOND SUNDAY OF LENT

Genesis 12:1-4a; psalm 32
2 Timothy 1:8-10; Matthew 17:1-9

Answering God's Call

T HROUGHOUT the years of his public ministry Jesus allowed the power of his Godhead to be seen in his miracles; but only on the one occasion, recorded in today's gospel, did did he allow a hint of its glory to be seen by anyone. Only the chosen few, the most intimate of his disciples, saw anything of the numinous aspect of his dual nature. That revelation was to give them strength when he was put to death apparently abandoned by God and man. The effect it had on them was to make them wholly indifferent to anything but to remain there in the presence of God. They were awed, they were frightened, but they were not so dismayed as to want to hide or to leave; they found the experience so attractive that all they wanted to do was to prolong it by setting up an encampment to make it permanent. That gives one some idea of how readily people would have followed him, if they had caught even a glimpse of his glory. It is not just that people are always seduced by signs and wonders, but rather if they are given a taste of heaven they are overwhelmed by it.

The miracles which Jesus did were often private, rather than public, manifestations of his power, they are nearly all miracles of healing; when they did take place in public they often had the consequence of making people want to turn him into a popular political leader, so that he was forced to escape from the crowds to avoid distortion of his mission. He worked to teach people the way to heaven within the limits of their ordinary lives. The only occasion when he was publicly acknowledged as King of the Jews, was when he was dying on the cross, in a final act of love. He opened the gates of heaven through his death and resurrection, offering salvation to all men who followed his teaching and who strove to do the will of God. The story of the transfiguration tells us more about the way in which he did not want to conquer men's hearts than about the way in which he chose to do so.

Faith has to do with trust in a God as we know him through his teaching and continued presence among us concealed in the bread and wine of the Eucharist. Faith is a mystery, a gift which we can accept or refuse, not a direct experience of the divine which would brook no denial.

Faith is not a set of propositions to which we give placid assent for half an hour on Sunday; it is a commitment of our lives to God. In the first reading today we are reminded of the story of Abraham, the archetypical man of faith; he did the will of God without counting the cost. He did not just leave home because God told him to, he spent his entire life faithful to God even when it seemed to mean that he must kill his only son, Isaac, to do God's will. God spared him that ordeal, but only when he had tested his faith to the limit.

We have been called to be holy, we have been given the gift of faith and the grace to bear the hardships of our journey through life. Lent is a time when we should review our lives and see how much surplus baggage we have accumulated which might interfere with our pilgrimage. Abraham left much that he valued behind when he answered God's call and set out for the uncertainties of the nomadic life. We are repeatedly warned in the gospels that the cares and preoccupations of the world will distract us from the call to follow Christ. We may easily become so busy and so caught up in the incessant demands of our daily lives that we lose sight of spiritual goals and values. It is wise therefore to re-establish our priorities and create space in our lives for Christ. It is not enough to give up some trifling luxury and think that we have dealt with Lent; the call to holiness may require more drastic sacrifice.

Lent should be an unsettling time, because being settled may be a type of spiritual inertia. It is not always easy to know what God wants of us, but unless we are open to God, and attentive to his call we are not likely to hear his voice. It is in prayer and recollection we find his will for us and the grace to follow his guidance.

The story of the transfiguration tells us both how easy it would be leave everything behind if we experienced the Godhead directly but also that this is not the way God chose to come into the world. The message the disciples received was that they were to listen to Jesus, to heed his teaching; the message is still the same.

Monica Lawlor

THIRD SUNDAY OF LENT

Exodus 17:3-7; psalm 94
Romans 5: 1-2, 5-8; John 4:5-42

Waters of Freedom

T HE WHOLE of the lenten season is reminiscent of the journey that people throughout the ages have made in search of God. Today's readings bring us stories from opposite ends of the scriptural spectrum with which most of us can readily associate. On the one hand, the people whom God had already delivered from slavery and chosen as his very own were the first to bring him to account for the way he was handling the journey. Hard hearts are faithless as well as forgetful. On the other hand, the woman at the well, who secretly searches for the Lord, suddenly stumbles across him in an everyday occurrence of her life.

Thirst is something which can divide as well as unite people. As a physical need it conjures up the most horrific pictures in our mind and can produce the most passionate responses. Indeed renal colic is the worst pain known to man. Some have even killed to satisfy their thirst. Later on in his gospel, John tells us that *sitio* is one of the very last words used by Jesus himself as he hangs upon the cross. Thirst needs to be satisfied.

The major challenge at both Massah and Meribah, and Jacob's well was to find the hidden stream of God's life which was being offered. On the surface, the people in the wilderness and the woman at the well were seemingly, searching for things other than God.

The gospel account of the Samaritan woman is a domestic scene and yet one of the most profound pieces of scripture. The location of the encounter with Jesus is an interesting one. The well had been purchased by the patriarch Jacob shortly after the famous wrestling match during which he had come to terms with God. It was through deception that Jacob inherited the birthright which belonged to his brother and thus became the father of the twelve tribes of Israel. This character weakness is in a way present in the Samaritan woman too, who was to be the first gentile to receive God's new inheritance, a revolutionary covenant that was to extend beyond Abraham's physical posterity. God is portrayed as showing the highest sensitivity towards the human condition in both these characters. A reminder to us perhaps of how he uses the weak to confound the strong, and of how all things cooperate in bringing about good.

In this context it is important to note that the woman was collecting water at a most unusual time of day. Water was generally collected in the early morning and again in the evening. This was to avoid the intense heat of the midday sun. It is also interesting to note that Jacob's well was at least half a mile outside the village which was built around its own well. The Samaritan woman was collecting water during the day in order to avoid meeting the other women of the village who gathered together at these times and who perhaps taunted or even shunned her because of her past. Such ridicule would have been an uncomfortable experience for anyone, but would have been made particularly unbearable if such derision came from people of high-minded religious intolerance. The noon-day sun would have been of little discomforture in comparison.

It is really wonderful to see how the relationship between Jesus and this woman grows as they converse. Throughout their exchange Jesus leads her to true conversion by opening her eyes. While her spirit may have been dampened by the words of others her heart had certainly not hardened itself against God. Being a woman who had been wronged she was a passionate searcher for the truth. As she approaches the well she is also approaching the fount of life.

During the course of what begins as humorous banter, Jesus is able to see within her as clearly as he would have been able to see into the heart of the well. Slowly but surely the intimacy between them grows. At first she is evasive when confronted with his personal observations about her life, but after retreating momentarily she is encouraged through this knowledge to become even more bold with him. Mindful of the prophecies of Ezekiel and the celebration of the Feast of Tabernacles in Jerusalem when vast amounts of water freely flowed through the Temple, the evangelist prompts her to remind Jesus of the exclusivity of Jewish worship. He sees deep into her heart. She recognises immediately that the conversation here is different from that which would be taking place had she drawn water from the village well. Jesus was offering her living water which would bring with it true freedom despite all that she had done.

While it is true that salvation comes to us from the Jews, Paul reminds us in his letter to the Romans that Jesus is the new temple of God's presence and that faith is the key to the temple gate. He himself speaks of the living waters of God's love which have been poured into our hearts by the Holy Spirit. For in the New Covenant water flows no longer from the well or the temple but from the very heart of Christ who draws all people to himself as he hangs upon the cross. This new and living water is offered to us as refreshment for the journey that leads us all to the Father whom we worship in spirit and in truth.

Arthur Roche

FOURTH SUNDAY OF LENT

1 Samuel 16:1, 6-7, 10-13; psalm 22
Ephesians 5:8-14; John 9:1-41

Discipleship

I T'S THIS theme which always takes over my mind every time I read the magnificent, indeed dramatic, story of today's gospel. The actual miracle fades into the background, is drowned in the noise of the debate.

Two groups, Jesus and the man, who was born blind, make up the debate. One group, his neighbours, really act upon a straighforward curiosity, mixed of course with a certain amount of first unbelief and, then wonder. They end up wanting to know where Jesus is. It would be wrong to suggest that the whole issue is totally uncrucial for them. But, somehow, you know the story teller is not really concerned with them. Indeed the man born blind seems to shrug them off.

When, however, the next group, the Pharisees, take the stage the whole event gets very serious, indeed, it gets nasty. For they want to question the fact that he has been healed at all. The real reason for the stand they take is found in the reply of the man born blind to their questioning: 'He is a prophet'. They begin using their doubts about the very fact of his previous blindness to undermine, indeed, not even to face,the reality of Jesus as prophet. The man's parents are called in and obviously don't want to get too involved with the whole business. At this point the Pharisees return to the man himself and he begins to get a little smart. To be honest, I can always hear, in my imagination, the crowds laughing. The key to what is happening, however, is in the words of the cured man to the Pharisees, when he asks, 'Do you want to become his disciples too?' This was too much for this theological elite. They link the man's blindness with his sin, they attack the credentials of Jesus. Then we are back with Jesus and back with Jesus face to face with one who, unlike the other groups, simply gives himself up to belief and discipleship. The end of the story is very neat. It turns blindness being attributed to sin into sin being attributed to an unwillingness to see.

Is it not all a picture of our world, as we search for how and where and in what God is being revealed to us? Of course, when we speak of discipleship we understand it in terms of discipleship of Jesus; but Jesus revealed, or the vision of Jesus revealed, in the world and human relationships, which make up our lives. When we all argue and debate at the politically, socially and theologically windswept street corners of our times, seeking God and life's meaning, the conversations go sour because of a terrible unwillingness, too often in us all, to face up to certain truths.

God reveals to us, I would think, the impossibility of discipleship, of the implentation of Jesus's vision, of the establishment of the Kingdom of holiness, justice, truth and love, in the violence of oppression, inequality, racism, poverty and intellectual elitism. These are the realities. Of course, there is a world of love and wonder and joy. But it is the sin of our blindness we must consider. Our unwillingness to see, in all its nakedness, what is wanting, where the failures are and, indeed, how we are all part of an act of terrible collaboration.

Our discipleship in the Lord and with each other offers us such a wonderful starting place. Even if we do not always agree, there can be no place for an unwillingness to see, in the communion of our discipleship. We anoint each other with love and truth; with gentleness and peace; and, crucially, with honesty in our common shared search to see the Lord revealed in our times. 'Try to discover what the Lord wants of you, having nothing to do with futile works of darkness but exposing them by contrast'. To be sure, this is not easy. But in the discipleship of Jesus we are not alone. Our discipleship should teach us not only to communicate to the world, it must also teach how to exist with, suffer with and even act with the world. Indeed, such existence and suffering and action are fundamental to any communication of truth. Is not this the whole meaning of, the Word made Flesh, which we reverence and identify with at all our gatherings?

Do you want to become
his disiples, too ?

Austin Smith

FIFTH SUNDAY OF LENT

Ezekiel 37:12-14; psalm 129
Romans 8: 8-11; John 11:1-45

The Spirit of God will Set you Free

I N THE first reading from today's mass, we receive a most dramatic vision of the power of the Spirit 'I am now going to open your graves; I mean to raise you from your graves, my people, and lead you back to the soil of Israel. . . And I shall put my spirit in you, and you will live . . . it is the Lord who speaks'. Dramatic though this vision may be, it only represents the insistent message of our God from the beginning of time if only we had ears to hear: the waters of chaos were transformed into the wonders of creation; we become living beings, from the moment when God breathes his spirit into us; the Israelite, placing their faith in the Lord, came safely through the waters of the red sea; wherever there is breakdown in God's handiwork, the Spirit is present to renew and create again.

This same Spirit, St Paul tells us, has made his home in us; together we belong to the body of Christ. And therefore, we are called to be a people of hope, a people always ready to heal, rebuild, to restore and replant; a people always believing in the possibilities of God. But do we believe in the power of this Spirit deep within us? Our lives are constantly threatened by the darkness of suffering and absurdity. We can hardly bear to think for long of the mental anguish of the parents of the young people slaughtered in cold blood in Northern Ireland; the Gulf War of 1991 doesn't seem to have brought peace any closer when we reflect upon the continuing plight of the Kurdish people; in the Holy Land, where Jesus lived, died and rose again, fear and hatred continue to divide people; and in Africa, we hear of millions of people on the verge of death by starvation. We live in a world in which we are surrounded by news of suffering and death. And within each one of us there is the constant experience of failure and weakness: the reminder that we are on the way to death. Faith in the power of the life-giving Spirit within us can seem so hollow.

And yet today we are called to proclaim the goodness of our world, a goodness which will most certainly come out on top. Not because of a mindless optimism, but because God has visited our world and told us so: 'I am the resurrection and the life. If anyone believes in me, even though he dies he will live, and whoever lives and believes in me will never die'. In Jesus, life wherever it was to be found was always passionately confirmed and accepted by God. This was especially true of the lives of those people who were so frequently considered to be utterly powerless: the sick, the handicapped, the elderly and the dying – people considered dead by those around them. Jesus went even further: when the human response was struck dumb, or, as happened so frequently during his life, was reduced to mocking laughter, he raised Lazarus his friend after four days in the tomb.

It is difficult for us to understand such an incredible happening in the life of Jesus but, in a dramatic way, it speaks to us of a life that knows no bounds and considers no situation beyond redemption. Jesus could well have reached Lazarus while he was still sick but he chose to stay where he was for two more days before proceeding to Judea. Indeed, Jesus leaves no doubt as to his reasons for delaying: 'Lazarus is dead; and for your sake I am glad I was not there because now you will believe. But let us go to him'. When they arrived, they found that Lazarus had already been in the tomb for four days; he was now beginning to smell and a heavy stone was placed against the opening of the cave. Inside Lazarus was bound and buried. Jesus would seem to be faced with impossibility in its most acute and final form.

But not quite! Jesus knew of the possibilities of the Spirit within him: 'Our friend Lazarus is resting, I am going to wake him... your brother will rise again'. And so Jesus approaches the tomb and cries out in a loud voice: 'Lazarus, here! Come out!' The dead man comes out of the grave, his feet and hands bound. and Jesus says to those standing by: 'Unbind him, let him go free'. All who came into the company of Jesus experienced him as life and resurrection.

This story of the raising of Lazarus inevitably reminds us of the experience that was shortly to overwhelm Jesus himself. Like Lazarus Jesus was bound and led from the garden (Jn 18: 12); and Annas sent him still bound to Caiaphas the highpriest. A few moments before he died, he, cried out in genuine anguish: 'My God, my God, why have you forsaken me?'. In that moment Jesus experienced for himself despair, anguish, emptiness and darkness; there seemed to be nothing more but to bind his body according to the burial custom of the Jews and place him in a tomb. But, as with Lazarus, God insists on the unbinding of Jesus: 'On the first day of the week. . . they found the stone rolled away from the tomb, but when they went in they did not find the body... (but) the linen cloths by themselves (Lk 24:1-12).

To the end, the message is an insistent one: our God is an unbinding God, a God who sets free. Do we, or do we not, believe this?

Peter Wilkinson

PALM SUNDAY

Isaiah 50:4-7; psalm 21
Philippians 2: 6-11; Matthew 26: 14-27, 66

Loyal in Love and Service

T ODAY'S readings present a wealth of themes for our reflection. As
Jesus comes to Jerusalem, to the holy city of the promise, we
recall the way he entered it and, with our own processions and palms,
we commit ourselves to follow him there. We undertake to come to the
mysteries of the passion which we celebrate throughout Holy Week not
simply as spectators, but as participants in the sacred mysteries of our
redemption. Jesus himself is our sole redeemer. He faced Jerusalem both
as priest and as victim, both voluntarily sacrificing himself and passively
offering himself for the salvation of our world. And as we begin to walk
in the footsteps of our great high priest we turn to the scriptures to
know how best to do this.

There are role models of course, characters from the gospel text who
show us what it means to seek to follow Jesus as he prepares for death.
Some of them give us a good example – Matthew singles out Mary of
Magdala, Mary the mother of James and Joseph and the mother of
Zebedee's sons, for instance. Then there are Peter and Judas, who are
somehow mirror images of each other, Caiaphas and Pilate who are
drawn unwittingly into the tale, rather like Simon of Cyrene. There are
the bystanders, the hostile crowd, the crowd of disciples who should
have been supportive – but in the event had found the whole thing too
much to bear. Each of these furnishes us with an insight into what it
means to follow Jesus; each of these reminds us of the gap between our
own loftiest ideals and the reality of a rather patchy performance.

So today let us focus on the characters from the gospel text who did
find the resources to be loyal in their love and service of the Lord.
Matthew's text is quite clear: 'And many women were there, watching
from a distance, the same women who had followed Jesus from Galilee
and looked after him'. Certain details emerge. We are not talking about
individuals but about a group, about people who found that
companionship made the impossible happen. Together they could take
their place where no individual could stand. Both Peter and Judas, we
cannot but notice, sinned as much by trying to take all the blame
personally as they did by denying Jesus in the first place. The women
who watched Jesus die however, did so as a group, supporting and
consoling both him and each other.

They watched from a distance. Are we to read this as a gesture of cowardice or realism? Would the more devout thing have been to move closer to the cross of Jesus? Or do the truly devout know their limitations? Know how far they can go and when they should hold back? And in any case draw comfort from the presence of Mary, the mother of Jesus and the Beloved Disciple at the foot of the cross.

The gospel text goes on to tell us that these are women who had 'followed Jesus from Galilee and looked after him'. The figure on the cross is one they recognise because they have followed him in love and in service. On the cross they can now recognise the image of love and of service taken to the limits. When the text from Philippians recalls that Jesus emptying himself to assume the condition of a slave and then becoming humbler yet by accepting death on a cross, it reminds us of something the women disciples of Jesus already knew about because of their own experience. Hence their presence at the death of Jesus. For them at least he was the only role model. They recognised themselves in him.

Evangeline Booth, whose experience of poverty and hardship earlier this century gave her the authority to write about the contemporary face of the dying Christ, noted in 1930:

On that first Good Friday, when all the apostles had forsaken the crucified Christ and fled from the scene of his redeeming agony, it was the women who were last seen at the cross, watching him there; and on the morn of resurrection, when the night was still unlit by the first hint of the brightest dawn in history, the women were not afraid to risk the perils of those riotous streets and make their way, loyally and modestly and reverently, to the silent tomb. It was in the body of a woman that Christ was born; and the souls of women were the cradles of the Church.
(Evangeline Booth, 'Woman', Fleming H. Revell Company, New York, 1930)

As we make our way – as women or as men – 'loyally and modestly and reverently' towards our celebration of the mysteries of the week we call holy, let us take inspiration from the lives of the holy women whose experience of love and service enabled them to follow the dying Jesus to the last.

Lavinia Byrne

MAUNDY THURSDAY

Exodus 12:1-8, 11-14; psalm 115
1 Corinthians 11:23-26; John 13:1-15

Christ's Way of Service

A LARGE painting entitled, 'The Washing of Feet', attributed to Tintoretto and belonging to the Chapter of the Cathedral Church of St Nicholas, Newcastle, is presently housed at the Shipley Art Gallery in Gateshead. The scene depicts a room of considerable proportions with Christ's disciples sitting around a table on stools or lounging on the floor. One apostle is shown pulling off his companion's stockings, another is replacing his sandal. The impression is of a relaxed and informal occasion.

The lower right hand corner of the canvas shows a reluctant Peter with one foot in a wash tub being ordered by Christ to put his other foot in as well. Peter's right hand is raised in a gesture of shocked defiance. It seems from the expression on his face that he cannot comprehend what is happening. The difficulty for him, and for the others present, was that in those times the leader of a group did not assume the posture and practices of a slave, one of whose tasks was to wash the dust from his master's feet as he entered the house. Peter's first, and perhaps typically impetuous, reaction in this situation was to refuse to allow the action to proceed.

Tintoretto's interpretation of the Last Supper is set against a background of informality and suggests that those present had little idea of the real significance of the event. The same impression is given in today's gospel. In spite of the warnings they had been given, it seems that Christ was alone in knowing that this occasion would be the last he would spend with his disciples before the momentous events of Calvary took place.

How would we mark such a moment: the last hour or so with our closest companions before a certain death? What memories would we want to leave with them? Perhaps we would give away some of our prized possessions or leave some final instructions, or even discuss the structure of our funeral liturgy. None of these things was appropriate for Christ. He wanted to mark the occasion as the summation of his ministry, to direct attention away from himself towards the kind of lifestyle he expected his friends to adopt after he had left them.

In the way of service, as demonstrated by Jesus, the master becomes the servant, an approach to interpersonal relationships which turns the usual values of society upside down. Conventional social behaviour would expect Christ, as group leader, to seek status and power. Instead, he takes the opposite course and assumes the mantle of the lowly by serving those in his care. In such manner, he sets the standard for the new community he is to leave behind after the resurrection. It would be a community in which service, sacrifice and sharing play central roles, attitudes of mind and heart symbolised by the washing of the feet.

This way of service is a unique expression of Christ's character and personality, and one which an outside observer, schooled in the precepts of Christianity, would expect to find among the values of those who followed him. In fact, there are many images of the servant described in the accounts of the events surrounding the passion and death of Christ but, significantly perhaps, all the incidents involve people outside Christ's immediate circle. It seems that the Apostles had disappeared and apart from his mother and the Beloved Disciple, others were left to follow the example initiated by Jesus: Simon of Cyrene, the good thief, Joseph of Arimathea, Nicodemus, Mary of Magdala, Salome, Joanna and other women observers who stood watching from a distance.

One of the criticisms directed at practising Christians is that they can appear to be less caring than others in society. Of course this is not true for everyone, but faced with the dramatic events of this liturgical season, each of us must ask ourselves how well we exercise the selfless service of Christ in our own lives.

Like Simon, and faced with daily frustration and perhaps suffering, we are urged to take up Christ's cross as our own and walk with him. Like the good thief and condemned alongside Christ for our sins, or like the women who observed from a distance, we must watch in prayer with Jesus and share his last moments. Like Joseph of Arimathea, who asked for Christ's body, we must be constantly on the alert for opportunities to assist others beyond the call of duty. Like Nicodemus, who provided the oils to anoint Christ's body for burial and resurrection, we can offer those in need the consolation of the healing balm of our compassion, forgiveness and love. Like the women who visited the tomb, we can respond to the requirements of others by going out of our way to give generously either our time or precious possessions.

In any of these ways we can show our true commitment to the service exemplified by Christ when he washed his disciples' feet. Paradoxically, by so doing we will be released from the slavery of a selfish attachment to our own needs. Moving out of our own limited world frees us for the new life promised by God when he freed the Israelites from slavery by the blood of a lamb and when he raised Christ from death on the first Easter morning.

David Watson

GOOD FRIDAY

Isaiah 52:13-53:12; psalm 30
Hebrews 4:14-16, 5:7-9; John 18:1-19: 42

New Life in the Spirit

AT THE CRUCIAL moment in his trial before Pilate, Jesus proclaims: 'Yes, I am a king. I was born for this, I came into the world for this: to bear witness to the truth.' Everything Jesus did bore witness to the truth; everything which happened to him gave witness to the truth. Even his dreadful suffering and deadth bore witness to the truth. As we reflect today on Christ's Passion we must ask ourselves the question 'how does the Passion bear witness to the truth?' Pilate asked Jesus 'what is truth?' The question he should have asked, and the question we must ask, is 'who is truth?'

Truth is not a thing. The truth that Jesus is bearing witness to is a person. While speaking about his return to the Father, Jesus said 'I am the Way, the Truth and the Life' (Jn 14:6). Jesus is the truth. He is the revelation of God. He said to his disciple 'to have seen me is to have seen the Father'(Jn 14:10). The truth to which Christ bears witness is the truth of God's immense love for us. The revelation of this love is the very heart of the good news which Christ preached. Witnessing to God's great love for us has brought Jesus to the point of laying down his life for us. We can easily miss the whole meaning of the Lord's Passion if we fail to see Christ's suffering and death as his supreme and ultimate witness to the truth of God's universal and all-forgiving love. The Pharisees did not believe in this universal love of the merciful Father. They believed that God loved them conditionally, because they 'kept the law'! But the rest, the sinners who were 'outside the law', were presumed not to be loved by God.

Jesus took the side of the sinners. He preached to them the good news that salvation is God's gift and not a human achievement. He went further. He said that we sinners will be saved not through our own good works, but by believing in himself. In the ears of his enemies, these were outrageous claims to make. And so they decided to kill him. If Jesus had 'toned down' his preaching he would not be standing before Pilate. But neither would he have borne witness to the truth. He would have been a king who had betrayed the truth! Witnessing to the Father's great love inevitably led Jesus into conflict with the authorities. God the Father didn't *will* Jesus to suffer such a death. As Jesus himself said, 'God sent his Son into the world not to condemn the world, but so that through him the world might be saved' (Jn 3:17). But the world will not accept the message. If Jesus delivers the message of God's love and salvation he will be killed; if he refuses to deliver the message he will be unfaithful to God. That was the dilemma. From the moment his own people rejected him and his teaching, his death was inevitable. All the prophets had foretold that 'the Christ must suffer'. When the Father said to him, as the Holy Spirit descended on him after the baptism, 'you are my Son, the Beloved' Jesus knew that he would have to suffer.

The 'Beloved' was the suffering Servant we hear about in the first reading from the prophet Isaiah. The devil had tried to use this knowledge to tempt him during his forty-days' fast. But now the hour has come. Just before he left for the garden of Gethsemane Jesus said 'Father, the hour has come, glorify your Son, so that your Son may glorify you' (Jn 17:1). Jesus is now ready to bear his ultimate witness to the truth of God's great love and lay down his life for our salvation. We are at the heart of the mystery of our redemption. As Isaiah foretold 'He was pierced through for our faults, crushed for our sins. On him lies a punishment that brings us peace, and through his wounds we have been healed' (Is 53: 5).

We find it very hard to comprehend the connection between Christ's suffering and the forgiveness of our sins. But we proclaim that connection every time we say our Creed: 'For our sake he was crucified under Pontius Pilate, he suffered death and was buried'. All that happened to Jesus was 'for our sake'. We are not asked to comprehend this mystery in our minds but we are asked to believe it in our heart.

Today we are asked to take the Passion of Christ to heart and say 'he was pierced through for my faults, crushed for my sins.. by his wounds I am healed'. The best way for us to gratefully celebrate Good Friday is to allow Our Lord to give us peace, to forgive us our sins, to heal our wounds and to fill us with the new life of the Spirit which he wants us to have.

Jim McManus

THE EASTER VIGIL

Genesis 1:1-2:2; psalm 103 or 32 Genesis 22:1-18; psalm 15;
Exodus 14:15-15: 1; psalm Exodus 15:1-6, 17-18;
Isaiah 55:1-11; psalm Isaiah 12:2-6; Baruch 3:9-15, 32-4:4;
psalm 18; Ezekiel 36:16-17a, 18-28; psalms 41 and 42;
Romans 6:3-11; psalm 117; Matthew 28:1-10

Through Death to Life

I N DECEMBER 1875 the Deutschland sailed from Bremen bound for America. On board were five Franciscan sisters exiled by laws restricting the freedom of the Church in Germany as part of Bismark's *Kulturkampf.* On the night of the 7th, the ship was blown by a severe storm onto the sands off the Kent coast. Some 200 on board were drowned. The bodies of the sisters were taken to the Franciscan church in Stratford, East London, where Requiem Mass was celebrated. Moved by these events, the Jesuit, Gerard Manley Hopkins put pen to paper and gave us his poem, *The Wreck of the Deutschland.*

Vividly the force of the wind and waves is described, 'sitting Eastnortheast, in cursed quarter, the wind; Wiry and white-fiery and whirlwind-swivelled snow'.

The ship ran aground; beaten by the waves the nuns were drowned:

> *she struck not reef or rock*
> *But the combs of a smother of sand: night drew her*
> *Dead to the Kentish Knock;*
> *And she beat the bank down with her bows and the ride of her keel:*
> *The breakers rolled on her beam with ruinous shock; ...*
> *To the shrouds they took, – they shook in the hurling and horrible airs.*

Sombre thoughts for this happy night in which we rejoice in the risen Lord. Our joy is in His triumph over death, our celebration is in the waters of baptism and food of life.

Hopkins in his poem sees the death of the five sisters as symbols of the five wounds of Jesus the crucified.

> *Five! the finding and sake*
> *And cipher of suffering Christ.*

Powerful waves battering a ship to matchwood on a sandbank dramatically illustrate the awful destructive power of water. To the nuns and the other travellers, the seas brought death.

By contrast the pictures we have seen of the famine stricken parts of Africa leave us in no doubt that human beings cannot survive without water. People can survive painfully without food for some weeks; but without water we can only last for days. Water brings life and freshness to our lives and to the life of the world around us. Plants, trees, the grass in the park, all need water for life.

Tonight's liturgy flows with water. In the water of baptism we celebrate the life God gives us and that our life does not end in death. Life is victorious over death. Christ is risen. 'Death has no power over him any more'.

Hopkins's dramatic picture of the nuns drowning in the wreck of the Deutschland portrays them as ciphers of the suffering Christ, five precious wounds. They are taken by the water of death, they enter the tomb. But that is not the end.

'We believe that having died with Christ we shall return to life with him' (Reading 8).The nun

> was calling 'O Christ, Christ, come quickly!'
> The cross to her she calls Christ to her,
> christens her wild-worst
> Best.

Like the women in our Easter gospel, the sisters of the Deutschland, battered by the stormy waters, discovered the Lord. 'Do not be afraid' he says, for in death the Lord comes, as Hopkins puts it 'kindly but royally reclaiming his own'.

On this holy night we celebrate that death is not the end but a stage in our journey to fullness of life with God. Christ the Lord has conquered death. He has gone ahead of us. We will see him (Gospel). Now it is dark outside. Night has fallen. Faced with the dark fear of death and the loss of loved ones we proclaim around this altar: Christ has conquered death. There are wild storms that must endure in our lives; emotional crises, depression, marriage break-ups, unemployment, financial crises, and in the face of all these we celebrate in the waters of baptism: God is life.

So let him Easter in us this night, let him Easter in us day by day.

> Let him Easter in us, be a dayspring to the dimness of us,
> be a crimson-cresseted East,
> More brightening her rare-dear Britain, as his reign rolls.

Kieran Kettleton

EASTER SUNDAY

Acts 10:34, 37-43; psalm 117
Colossians 3: 1-4 or1 Corinthians 5: 6-8; John 20: 1-9

The Impact of the Resurrection

'**C**HRISTIANS, to the paschal victim offer sacrifice and praise. The sheep are ransomed by the Lamb'. Easter Sunday is one of those precious days in the year when the Mass liturgy contains a Sequence, a reflective song which is, at least in the Latin *Victimae paschali* of Wipo, a poetic masterpiece of theological and devotional compression. Here the opening words of the Sequence shock us with their paradox: we are called to offer sacrifice to a victim! Full-grown sheep, we are told, 'have been rescued by a lamb! It acts as a good introduction to the meaning of this greatest of all days in our annual cycle, because unless we come to glimpse something of the mind-blowing impact of Christ's resurrection upon its first witnesses and upon ourselves, we will never properly understand our faith.

Christ's resurrection in itself: what is it? A clue lies in the first reading, where the newly-invigorated St Peter witnesses to the resurrection with the words, 'We have eaten and drunk with him after his resurrection from the dead'. This surprisingly physical statement indicates that the resurrection was no mere 'spiritual experience', no mere affirmation that 'love triumphs over all'; it was the resurrection of the body itself. The incarnate Son, Jesus of Nazareth, rose from the grave in his human body; the same, yet different; no longer subject to death, no longer limited by time and space, and yet recognisably the same person; in a word, changed, transfigured, glorified.

But this glorification of Christ is no mere marvel to round off the Jesus story; it is a model, a foretaste, of what we ourselves are destined to go through. The whole of us, body and soul, is intended for God, not just the soul. The body is not intended for frustraion; it is a sacred vessel, a temple where God really dwells. Baptism, with its commitment to lead the new life of love, and with its gift of forgiveness of sins, actually begins the process of resurrection within us, a new creation, only completed at our final rising from death. This is why St Paul, in the passage from his letter to the Colossians, talks about us having already died and having already risen 'to true life with Christ'.

What are the consequences of this revolutionary seed of resurrection growing in us? Firstly, we have an obligation to live in a certain way, namely, to live out death-to-sin by giving 'the things of heaven' first place in a life that is 'hidden with Christ in God'. This hidden life implies leading such a life-style as will be beyond the sympathy and understanding of many of our fellow-men; it will be hidden also, in the sense that the fully-risen person we are meant to become will remain largely concealed until the final resurrection day. Two images offered by the New Testament to illustrate this hiddenness are those of the seed, hidden yet growing under the earth, and the yeast buried in dough, yet working away to raise the whole into finished bread. This is the picture hinted at by St Paul in the alternative reading from 1 Corinthians (though Paul uses the paschal unleavened bread to illustrate the 'newness' of the hidden life). Just as the final fruit and the finished bread only come at the end of a process, so the real 'me' will only be revealed at the completion of the raising process which God is effecting in my life.

So the resurrection not only gives us the key to understanding the mortal lives of Jesus and ourselves, it also changes our lives at the very centre, and empowers us to live in a new way. This new way is referred to in the reading from Acts. Jesus 'went about doing good', that is, he lived a life of selfless love. We too must live like this, otherwise the new life within us can atrophy and die. There is a kind of dying, we must be ready for, however. Just as Jesus' life of loving brought about his unpopularity and death, so our death, whether inflicted on us or not, must be the consequence of loving. 'Dying to sin', if persevered in, will come to a climax with a 'happy death', that is, a truly blessed one.

In the justly famous passage from St John's gospel, we are privileged to glimpse the first dawning of the notion amongst his friends that Christ is risen. It should not surprise us that it was John, 'the disciple Jesus loved', who first made the break-through; 'till that moment they had failed to understand. . . that he must rise from the dead'. The historical details given are not only authenticating, they are also profoundly moving: the picture of Mary Magdalen so beside herself that she failed to enter the tomb; the picture of the detailed arrangements of the grave linen in the tomb itself; the picture of John outrunning Peter, but allowing Peter to enter first. Our prime response, as we consciously place ourselves along with Peter and John in the ranks of believers, must be one of thanks and praise to the Father for such an unimaginable and amazing plan of salvation. 'This is the day that the Lord has made', says the Responsorial Psalm. Let us say with the sons of Israel, 'His love has no end!'

Aelred Burrows

SECOND SUNDAY OF EASTER

Acts 2:42-47; psalm 117
1 Peter 1:3-9; John 20:19-31

The Believing Thomas

P OOR THOMAS! Today's brilliant story has become so well-known that he features (even in Roget's *Thesaurus*) as the archetype of all doubters, disbelievers and sceptics. He's not even, like the central character of other gospel stories, allowed time off. This story of John's is down to be read each year, A, B and C .

Perhaps John succeeded too well. He was trying to tell us that no one can see that Jesus is risen without believing: 'Blessed are those who have *not* seen, and yet believe.' Un-blessed therefore the Pilates and Herods and Caiaphases who, whatever the evidence put before them, could never have accepted that the Jesus they had put to death was still alive . That needs faith. And if Thomas *did* eventually see Jesus (even if it took a long time for the denarius to drop) it can only be because he too had become a believer. People think seeing is believing. But in the case of the risen Christ, John is saying, believing is seeing.

To present this absolutely basic fact about the Easter Jesus, John turns (like all the biblical writers before him) to a story. The 'Doubting-Thomas' story is simply a more dramatic version of the 'Hesitant Magdalene' or of the 'Artless-Emmaus Pilgrims', or of the 'Carpetted-Disciples'. For the conviction that the crucified one still lives is not an easy one to come by. Even when such faith is achieved, it will always remain ambiguous, tinged with doubt, intermittent, 'Lord-I-believe-help-thou-my unbelief'.

And the gospel's purpose is to allow us to share and deepen this faith ('These stories have been recorded so that you may *believe*, and *believing* have life through his name'). It would be pointless to read them as video-recordings of long ago. Of what use would that be to my faith? I can't base my faith on a tomb I am told was found empty, or on visions people tell me they have seen. I can only base my faith on Jesus himself, when I know that he is alive because he makes it possible, day after day, to pass from death to life. And to support my faith in such a Jesus, I need to read these stories over and over again.

So I am grateful to John for giving me the Thomas story. I want to take it seriously — which is not to say literally. In fact literally, I would want to tell him that the character who actually sees the risen Christ, and physically touches him, is obviously more fortunate than me, who can 'only' darkly believe in him. Who would not opt to be Thomas rather than me?

John would presumably say, 'You are right. Of course what Thomas does in the story feels more real. But that is only because he is a character in a story. The story is deliberately dramatising the fact that the risen Christ is a reality, not an illusion. But outside the story, that fact can only be grasped by faith.'

Paradoxically therefore, the punch-line of the story is a plea not to take the story literally. Only those who do take it literally will imagine that Thomas is in a more fortunate position than they are. In the real world he is not. Thomas, like us, could only 'see' the risen Christ by believing in him. In the real world, believing that Christ is risen cannot mean physically touching him, whether we are talking of the first disciples of Jesus or the last. What a materialist view of our world, to think otherwise!

Today's epistle provides a striking comment on the elusiveness of the risen Christ. The opening chapters of Peter's letter have so many references to the Exodus, to a desert exile, to the death and resurrection of Jesus, and to a new birth, that many scholars think they are part of a first century baptismal homily, possibly delivered by Peter himself. Today we share the opening lines of this homily, which remind us of the meaning of our own baptism, and warn us that no follower of Jesus can avoid the ambiguity of the resurrection experience.

You've not seen him,
yet you love him,
The painful exile continues,
yet you're already full of inexpressible joy.
Salvation is still distant,
yet your treasure is safe in God's hands.
The risen Christ has not yet been revealed,
yet in faith you already hold him.

Those who have faith do indeed put their hand into the wounded side of the risen Christ whence flows the very Spirit that enables them to live like Jesus.

H. J. Richards

THIRD SUNDAY OF EASTER

Acts 2:14, 22-28; psalm 15
1 Peter 1: 17-21; Luke 24:13-35

In the Breaking of Bread

T HE RESURRECTION is hard to believe in. The gospels so often seem to involve events that could never happen to anyone we know, and which seem to belong to the world of fairy-tale and fable. Angels in shining garments, empty tombs, miraculous dawn appearances. In our world, in our time, the graves in which we place our loved ones do not give up their dead, there are no angels, we are granted no messengers from heaven to tell us that all shall be well, that the Lord is risen. We can't look at the place where they laid him, to see the stone rolled away, the grave-clothes empty. Even the Holy Shroud, has apparently turned out to be a mediaeval work of art!

It is tempting to think that between the miracle world of the scripture and our world there is a great gap, a gap which makes it harder to believe. Where there was once poetry and magic, there is only the cold light of humdrum reality.

Today's gospel offers us a picture of the reality of the resurrection which seems helps us to see that this is not so. Though many people would say it was the most moving and vivid of all the resurrection appearances of Jesus, there is no 'magic' here, no angels, no stones rolled away: there are not even any star performers, no apostles, no Mary Magdalene. Instead, there are just two people like ourselves, bewildered as we often are, their faith faltering. This is a story about doubt and loss of direction turned to strong and joyful faith, but it is not done by spectacular demonstration: the methods Jesus uses in this story are the ones he uses now. The men on the the road to Emmaus are ourselves.

The two disciples are on a journey away from Jerusalem: away from the Holy City, the place of revelation, and the scene of the saving events of Good Friday and Easter. Perhaps they were leaving the church, on their way back to a life in which there was no great hope, no promise of the Messiah, but where at least there would be no terrible disappointments, none of the desolation of Good Friday. Like us they are voyagers, unsure of their bearings, and night is drawing on. And when they encounter a stranger on the journey they don't recognise Jesus. They even get a little irritated at the apparent stupidity of his questions to them.

This is the turning point of the story, for Jesus, begins to teach them, leading them through the Jewish scriptures, to show how his life and death and rising really are the fulfillment of all that God's people had been waiting for. And his words reach their hearts: when they arrive at the village where they plan to spend the night, he makes as if to move on, but they hold on to him 'Stay with us, it is nearly evening'. They sit down to a meal. And now he does what he has done dozens of times with them before. Taking bread he blesses it and breaks it, and as he does so, 'their eyes were opened, and they recognised him', and he vanishes from sight.

This is a warmly human story, but we are not meant to think that it was the familiarity of friendship which tells them who he is. The blessing and breaking of the bread is not here just the start of a meal, it is the Eucharist, and they recognise him now not because of a familiar mannerism, but because he has opened their eyes by explaining the scriptures to them. If the story were just an anecdote about an appearance, you might expect the disciples to comment on the Lord's appearance, and to bewail his departure, but they do no such thing. There is no sense of disappointment, no worry that he has gone away. They are full of excitement and faith, as they remember his teaching: 'Did not our hearts burn within us while he talked to us on the road, while he opened to us the scriptures?' And now they know where they are and, more important, where they should be: they return at once to Jerusalem, to meet with the rest of the disciples, and to spread the good news that the Lord is alive.

Nobody knows exactly where the biblical village of Emmaus is: that is just as well, becuase it's importance is not that it is a place seven miles outside Jerusalem – in fact it is *every* place. The Lord who came to these dsiciples on their journey comes in the same way, now, to all of us, as we make our journeys through life. Like the men on the road to Emmaus, often we do not recognise him. But now, as then, we share his body together in the breaking of the bread. Here, Sunday by Sunday, however uncertain we are, however weak our faith or faltering our hope, is food for the journey, and companionship along the way. Here our hearts can respond to his word, to the promises of the kingdom he will bring, and we can work for. We will see no angels, but we do not need to, for the Lord is near, he is in the midst of us, he is known to us in the breaking of bread.

Stay with us, Lord Jesus, for it is nearly evening. Be our companion on the road: rekindle our hearts and stir up our hope, so that in the scriptures and in the breaking of the bread we and all our fellow men and women may learn to know you, the redeemer of Israel, the redeemer of the world. Amen.

Eamon Duffy

FOURTH SUNDAY OF EASTER

Acts 2:14, 36-41; psalm 22
1 Peter 2: 20-25; John 10:1-10

Ordinary People

T ODAY, we heard part of the first letter of Peter. A great deal of uncertainty surrounds this letter – when it was written, and by whom, exactly. Don't be put off by this – scholars have to examine our scriptures honestly and sincerely, in order to help us gain as much as possible from the truth they contain.

Most scholars agree that this letter was addressed to Christians who were finding it difficult to live according to their new-found faith within a very unsympathic world. So we find words of encouragement in this letter, along with advice on how best to deal with various situations. The part we heard today centres on the relationship between Christians and their worldly masters.

This brings us face to face with the reality of life for many early Christians. They weren't a separate group of believers who could look to their own numbers for strength and support. The church was in its infancy – believers might well find themselves quite isolated among the overwhelming mass of people for whom Jesus of Nazareth meant nothing.

Becoming a Christian might be sudden and unexpected. In today's first reading from Acts, Peter confronts ordinary people with the idea that Jesus, whom they had crucified, has been revealed as the Lord.

Let's not pass this point too quickly. This is the sort of scripture passage which some might use to show how Jewish people were responsible for the death of Jesus. They can reach salvation, of course, but only by repenting and turning to Jesus. It really is terribly important, given the sad history of the Jewish people right up to our own century, to lay this particular ghost.

No-one should be in any doubt that Jesus was killed by ordinary people. They certainly happened to be Jewish. But if Jesus appeared in our day, he might well be rejected all over again, but this time by Christians who, like their Jewish counterparts of two thousand years ago, don't want their boats to be rocked by some upstart who claims to be speaking for God.

Jesus was killed by ordinary people – people like us. Jesus wasn't killed by the Jewish people, while the rest were busy polishing our haloes. Jesus was killed by the people of the world. Each of us carries some responsibility for the rejection of Jesus – a rejection which is renewed each time our selfishness and brokenness bubble to the surface.

Anyway, in this reading from Acts, we find that many people, realising Jesus actually is the chosen one of God, want a second chance. That's no problem: it's never too late to accept the message of Jesus.

Now, back in the first letter of Peter, we find people who had indeed taken the Word of God into their lives, only to find themselves out on a limb. They have taken this new faith on board – they sincerely believe in Jesus – and their way of life has changed. Their attitudes and relationships, their hopes and fears, all have to be rethought in light of their new faith.

So we find the writer of the letter offering advice on how to get on with non-believers. Some Christians were employed by non-believers; some indeed were slaves. The writer tells them that, even when they are punished unjustly by those with power over them, they can turn the experience into something good. Jesus did not retaliate when people turned against him, despite his innocence. Here is an opportunity for ordinary believers to be like him, bearing patiently whatever life brings their way.

The writer is saying: don't be afraid – the world can do nothing to you, because Jesus is risen. 'Through his wounds you have been healed'. But it is not always easy to trust God totally. When the going gets rough, most of us feel the need to stand up for ourselves – you know, 'Praise the Lord, but pass the ammunition'! And yet, complete trust is asked for. Either God cares for us, or he does not.

Psalm 22, which we heard today, is the classical statement of God's love for all people, leaving no room whatever for any doubt. To the non-believer it's just a fairy tale; but for the believer, it brings a question which must be continually re-posed. Do I really trust God enough to believe all this?

In today's gospel, Jesus underlines the reality of the God's love for his people. The shepherd, says Jesus, goes ahead of his flock, and they follow because they recognise his voice and trust it. Anyone who enters the sheepfold cared for by the shepherd will be safe.

So, Jesus leaves us in no doubt about his and the Father's love and protection. The problem is that this love is for grown-ups. It's not the kind that makes promises to children who are frightened of the dark. This love and protection doesn't mean that there will be no pain, no suffering, no death. It mean that nothing in this life is of any consequence compared to what is to come – and that is guaranteed by Jesus. So, you see, this love asks us to respond with a very simple faith. Some people can manage to do that. And others? Others just can't – well, not today at any rate. But remember, it's never too late.

Colin Stewart

FIFTH SUNDAY OF EASTER

Acts 6:1-7; psalm 32
1 Peter 2:4-9; John 14:1-12

The Magnificent Seven

I N THE HISTORY of great campaigns and battles, it is the strategy, tactics and the fighting, which attract most interest. Less dramatic is the story subsequent to victory. After action, what follows? The care of the wounded, the security of the territory gained; its government, the placing of holding units, communications, care of civilians, There is a return to the purposeful ways of peace, the building up of morale and just administration. The blood and horror and waste of battle, in a just victory gives way to constructive rehabilitation.

'Sing my tongue, the glorious battle, sing the ending of the fray', we sing at Easter. Yes, but now the victorious little Church, in secretly victorious ways, is to consolidate, exploit its triumphant start. Today in our readings we are re-treading that path, with valuable, perennial lessons for us today. The church sets up her organisation by an ordination; she dwells on the fulfilment of prophecy, she sings in hope, she hears the assurance of the Master in the Gospel. After the battle of the cross and victory of the risen Christ, her head, the church attends to administration, establishes the doctrine of effective atonement, and finally St John, sublime as always, raises us to the to the very heart of the Trinity, in order that Christ's followers may do even greater works than himself – because he is going to the Father.

Indeed the scriptures display to us a businesslike, purposeful well-founded Church. In military parlance again, we see an effective regrouping, a stable organisation emerging, with morale high and the Lord's prophecy about himself fulfilled. Now on every side, our scriptures today should be our pattern; what they show of life in the Church of the late first century should inspire us in the late twentieth. So a little closer look will reveal the same sorts of people, the same solidity of doctrine, the same morale in the Spirit, the same Trinitarian life for the Church Militant and all her members; in short, the same Catholicism.

Spring 1991 saw in one great English diocese, the ordination of a score of men to the Sacred Diaconate. They bore names of scripture and names of today, just as the 'magnificent seven' of Acts 6, bore contemporary names. The commentator of the *Revised Standard Version* of the Bible declares: when all the critics have had their say: 'These are traditionally regarded as the first deacons'. Let's hear that roll-call again.

'The whole assembly,' we read 'approved this proposal, and elected Stephen, ...together with Philip, Prochorus, Nicanor, Timon, Parmenas, and Nicolaus of Antioch ....' Your commentaries, at home – or yet to be bought, or in your local library, are of profound interest, and do remember that commentaries of every level are now available for all tastes from the popular to the pedantic; so let us have a taste from one of them, about our section from Acts, Chapter 6, today, where the presentation of the seven to the apostles, and the laying on of hands, are observed.

The commentary records: 'The Jewish ritual expressed both transfer of function and bestowal of powers ... and it is an ecclesiastical practice of Luke's own time ... read back into the story of the Church's beginnings. It graphically expresses, for Luke, the subordination of this originally Hellenistic (Greek) leadership to Jesus's chosen apostles.'

So much for the church organisational. The church choral, in our psalm for today, refers in the last verse to the Lord, responding to us who revere him and hope in him. The psalm indeed leads into St Peter's teaching in the second reading, to remain close to the Lord, so that our offering may indeed be his – as it is in this very mass. And we see ourselves as living stones resting as it were on Christ the rock, the keystone. To sum up this imagery, we are reminded that we have the highest possible spiritual status, in the whole body to which we are joined; we are royal, and we are priests. I wonder if, when we pray privately again, we pray to God with that kind of claim on him may not the whole transaction become transformed?

It is the Alleluia, with its text from the gospel, which gives the note for the whole portion. Again, we have a magificent prayer motto which could be ours for the week. 'I am the Way, the Truth, and the Life. No one can come to the Father, except through me'. All the organising, the bustling life of the Acts; all the grasp of ancient prohecy and sacrifice, in Peter's letter – all depend on the real physical fact of the Son integrating the church and the human race into the life of the Trinity. The gospel includes, helpfully, a minor but important question-and-answer lesson between Jesus and Philip which keeps it thoroughly human.

What a treasure of preparation is ours today as we lead into the Ascension, Pentecost and Trinity! The hope and assurance of our Communion antiphon expresses it all: ' ... he who lives in me, and I in him, will bear much fruit.'

To refer back to my introduction: the victory of Christ is ours; we are to bear its fruit by establishing, consequent upon the victorious battle of the cross and resurrection, his kingdom of peace and love.

Bill Mason

SIXTH SUNDAY OF EASTER

Acts 8:5-8, 14-17; psalm 65
1 Peter 3:15-18; John 14:15-21

New Life, Old Thief

PROCRASTINATION, a good word in anybody's book, is the thief of time they tell us, and yet it is a thief that is often welcomed by us. We feel somehow in charge, somehow on top of things if we just let it go for another five minutes, another hour, another day, another week and so it goes on. There is a temptation for us to postpone. What is true in life is true in faith because one reflects the other. Procrastination can effect our spiritual lives as well, as we delay our response to the demands of belief and play for time with God. This temptation is particularly acute with the demands of new life which the Easter season puts before us. Sometimes we postpone our Easter until it is too late.

Let me explain, there is a tendency to postpone new life till after death. There is a temptation to wait till we are dead before we live. Easter gives us the possibility of new life, it invites us to live the resurrection but sometimes we think that we've got to be dead before we live. We say 'Jesus is risen, that means I can have eternal life' or 'Easter means that the followers of Jesus have eternal life'. Yes, all these things are true, but they also miss the point that Easter means new life for *today*, for now. Eternal life and Easter are connected, they are connected by our lives. The new life is for living, not for waiting until we are dead. One of the greatest mistakes we could make, one of the most drastic delays we could imagine, is to postpone life until we are dead.

Had Jesus ascended to heaven immediately after his resurrection and stayed there then we could be forgiven for thinking the new life of Easter was only for us after we got to heaven. But he didn't, he stayed on earth and he spoke to his followers about the new life. He taught them and gave them the gifts they required to live that new life – those same gifts are given to us. The new life is for us today, and tomorrow and the next day, it is for living, not for waiting until we are dead. Take a look at the gospels which we have been hearing over the past few weeks of the Easter season, the gifts that Jesus gives are the tools for the new life. He gives peace, forgiveness, both the knowledge that we are forgiven and the knowledge that we have the possibility to forgive. He gives and promises the Holy Spirit, who will be the one who makes forgiveness possible and the one who opens our minds to understand the scriptures and finally he gives us a mission, both personally to keep his word and commands and as a group to make his ways and his love known in our world. These are the gifts of the new life and these are things which are useless in heaven but useful for the here and now. These are the tools of the new life, these are the things which make the new life possible and necessary now.

Look at the progress which the *Acts of the Apostles* charts for us, we see the mission of the apostles, the power of their actions as well as the power of their witness and preaching. We see the gift of the Holy Spirit who empowers and encourages. All these are the parts of the new life which we postpone at our peril. We can imagine arriving at the pearly gates ready to begin the new life and finding out that we have missed our chance. The gifts are offered, the empowering is offered and the opportunity is offered, all these things can be stolen from us by only one thief, by procrastination. Easter is celebrated as a feast of new life, it is a feast best celebrated by living, by living a life that is new. Clearly this is news to make us happy and the psalm puts it in a nutshell;

> *Cry out with joy to God all the earth*
> *O sing to the glory of his name*
> *O render him glorious praise*
> *Say to God: 'How tremendous your deeds!'*

Here is the crux, not only is all this true, it is true for us – we are the ones given the tools and the invitation to live the new life. This hasn't happened sometime in the past and destined not to happen to us in our lifetime. It is a reality for us, a practical invitation from the Lord to understand his commands and to live them with the power of the Spirit alive within us. This is the promise which we inherit – that the Spirit will be with us to empower us to live this new life, which is not postponed for any reason. No temptation can persuade us to postpone our participation in the new life. There is no procrastination for us who recognise the action of the advocate in our midst. Procrastination will be for us neither the thief of time nor the thief of life, neither the new life for now or the eternal life to come.

Michael McMahon

THE ASCENSION

Acts 1:1-11; psalm 46
Ephesians 1:17-23; Matthew 28: 16-20

Heaven and Earth

C HRIST'S own presence now, and the present life of the Christian in this world are well expressed and illustrated by today's feast. On the one hand it celebrates his departure from us, the absence of his tomb and bones among us: 'The Lord goes up with shouts of joy'. His earthly work is at an end. He has gradually brought his own to the point of being able to understand that the kind of bodily presence which they had enjoyed throughout his earthy ministry is not the final or the only way he can be with them. 'He had shown himself alive to them after his Passion by many demonstrations: for forty days he had continued to appear to them and tell them about the kingdom of God,' Now it was all over and he could, as it were in one sense, afford to leave them. His departure from them, like that of the prophet Elijah (2 Kings 2:1-13) left his followers downcast; for it was a true departure. He was now in a position of power 'made to sit at God's right hand in heaven, far above every Sovereignty, Authority, Power and Domination'. This last text brings home to us the fact that his power is not to be measured simply in terms of his presence, especially his bodily, Palestinian presence.

Yet this sense of disappointment at the seeming absence of Christ after his ascension should not obscure our awareness of the reality of his presence then and now. Once we have freed our mind of spacial imagery and come to realise that heaven is more of a state than a place, we can come to see God as very real to us now. In other words Christ's physical absence is amply compensated for by his promise of perpetual presence till the end of the age (Matt 28:20). Christ's invisible 'sitting in heavenly places' is balanced by his presence 'when two or three are gathered together in his name' (Matt 1:20); among the least of his 'little ones' (Matt 25:40) and as the bread of life in the Eucharist (Jn 6:53 ff).

To Christ's real absence and his new ways of being present correspond the differing attitudes of the believer. He is to walk with his head in the heaven and his feet on earth. The old collect for this feast prayed that as Christ our head had gone before us, we also might learn to dwell in heavenly places. Christ is our head and we are in him. Christ is in heaven; from there he is always ready to help us and to pray for us (Heb 7:25). From the moment of our baptism we are not free to reduce our awareness of ourselves to creatures with no hope and no interest beyond this present world.

But the apostles were warned by the two men in white not to allow their gaze to rest solely upwards. There was work to be done, a gospel to be preached 'throughout Judaea and Samaria and indeed to the ends of the earth'. The other-worldliness, which lies at the heart of the gospel should not allow the christian apostle to forget that his duty is to be worked out in the world in which he lives. On the other hand if the good Christian is not something of a sky pilot, it is only too easy to forget that the christian message and christian mission cannot be reduced to a purely this worldy business. Christ did not come to inaugurate a 'kingdom of this world' (Jn 18:36). He was tempted to do so both by the devil (Matt 4:9) and by the enthusiastic crowds (Jn 6:15). But he consistently rejected this perversion of his message. Following his master's example the christian can never feel completely at home in this world, for like Christ the Christian knows that despite his loyalty to the various kingdoms of this world, his citizenship and final home is already in heaven (Eph 2:19, Heb 11:13). Our final resting place is the 'heavenly Jerusalem, which is our mother (Gal 4:26). We have all to learn how to pass through the things of earth in such a way as not to lose those of heaven.

Anthony Meredith

SEVENTH SUNDAY OF EASTER

Acts 1:12-14; psalm 26
1 Peter 4:13-16; John 17:1-11

Asking the Real Questions

O NE OF my abiding memories as a kid was being told by my mother as I went to bed 'Don't forget to clean your teeth and say your prayers.' My prayers followed a rule similar to the law of thermal expansion and contraction of metals. If the bedroom was warm my prayers were longer. As the temperature dropped so my prayers shortened. In the bleak midwinter God got very short measure. My faith in the power of prayer was shattered at an early age. In my teens I became aware of a very pretty girl at our church and, in order to secure her favour, I said the 'Thirty Day' prayer for the prescribed period. This prayer was guaranteed to work, and so great was my faith that I ringed the thirty first day on the calendar and prayed on. After a month I was rattling through it in seconds. However there must have been some small print in the guarantee that I had missed, for the lady remained aloof. Although I still said my prayers and cleaned my teeth I began to wonder what Jesus meant when he said 'Ask and you shall receive'. My prayer life became moribund though my teeth grew in virtue (perhaps I should have tried dental prayer).

The 'penny catechism' has come in for much criticism but its definition of prayer is perfect – the raising up of the mind and heart to God. The success of our prayer will depend on how we see God. My view was that he was a rather bad tempered old man who could be wheedled into changing his mind. My view of him has been shared by many, not least the authors of the prayers in the Roman Missal used until the sixties. The prayer in time of famine reads ... 'may men acknowledge in their hearts that such scourges spring from thy wrath and cease by thy mercy'. If we see God as an angry God who is punishing the innocent people of the starving world because of his anger our prayers to him will be little different to those of the pagan, who tries to appease a volcano with human sacrifices. Two of the readings today are about prayer – the prayer of Jesus at the Last Supper and the prayer of Mary and the apostles before Pentecost. The prayer of Jesus shows his intimacy with his Father. He prays for his own glorification so that the Church may receive the Holy Spirit. Mary and the apostles are praying for their own preparation for the gift of the Holy Spirit. This is the last time Mary is mentioned in the scriptures. It is fitting that she should be united with the apostles in prayer for she who is named as 'The Mother of Jesus', here is honoured as the Mother of the Church, present at its birth.

How then do we see God? Pascal, the 17th century French theologian, said that man has made God in his own image. We know that we can sometimes be persuaded to change our minds – not least by flattery (which is not the same thing as praise). So we see God like ourselves ready to change his mind if we keep up the honied words. However prayer changes us. It can't change God and so every prayer must be 'Your Will Be Done' which means a change in us, for we cannot say that we are ready for what we are praying for.

I feel a great deal of sympathy with the man who had the task of arranging a retreat for a men's organisation. He asked the priest to be practical and added 'the lads don't want any airy-fairy stuff on prayer'. Most of us are perfectly willing to 'say' prayers. That expression is part of our language but really it is not a good part for prayer springs from heart first, with or without the use of spoken words. Words give us something to get our teeth into, yet it is easy leave the heart out of our prayers. Praying without words seems 'airy-fairy'. In fact prayer is, for most of us, hard work. Martha had a wonderful way of dodging the hard work of raising up her mind and heart to God by hyper-activity. As a life long sufferer from Marthritis I have made that dodging an art....but Mary chose the better part.

Prayer has many expressions in the modern Church and there is no one way that is right at the expense of all others. Nobody is an expert in prayer. We can all learn and if we don't try to grow in our relationship with God our prayer will be trivial. We have all seen relationships that are loving in a way but without communication so often because of lack of will and effort. My prayer lacks will and effort. One person who understood prayer better than many was Anna, heroine of *Mister God This is Anna*. Anna was a little moppet of six who came to understand how trivial people are when they pray. Shortly before her death Anna prayed 'Please, Mr God, teach me to ask real questions'. She saw prayer as asking Mister God questions, and said that people asked him little questions and could only expect little answers. I think that she understood what Jesus meant when he said 'Ask and you shall receive'. Every prayer is answered – but then I get the answer I deserve. I must learn to ask real questions.

Richard Wilson

WHIT SUNDAY

Acts 2:1-11; psalm 103
1 Corinthians 12:3-7, 12-13; John 20:19-23

Semper Reformanda

The content of the Whitsun liturgy is rich, and that is also true of the Sunday Mass. The texts of the day show the Holy Spirit as present and active in the world, in the Church and in the heart of each Christian. In the world: 'The Spirit of the Lord fills the whole world' (entrance chant). The Spirit that hovered over the waters at the creation of the world is at work still. He 'renews the face of the earth' (psalm). The Holy Spirit is present in the Church (first and second readings and gospel) and he is present in each individual. This is emphasised especially in the Veni Sancte Spiritus, now generally credited to Stephen Langton, Cardinal and Archbishop of Canterbury who died in 1222. We find the same theme in the Prayer after Communion: 'Keep within us the vigour of your Spirit...' Obviously all these themes cannot be dealt with in a single homily but the texts of Years B and C offer opportunities to exploit other aspects of the liturgy of the day. In what follows I have chosen to speak of 'the completion of the Paschal Mystery' (Preface) as seen in the sending of the Holy Spirit on the Church.

FOR THE LAST seven weeks we have been celebrating the Paschal Mystery. Our thoughts have been much on Christ risen from the dead and on the Holy Spirit he promised to send. Today that season is brought to its conclusion with the sending of the Holy Spirit on the Church so that it could begin its mission to every nation on earth. By the sending of the Holy Spirit the Father 'brought the paschal mystery to completion'. We may have thought that the work of our redemption was completed on the cross, or perhaps by the resurrection. But that work has to continue throughout time and so the Spirit is sent upon the Church so that it could preach the good news of salvation to every creature and incorporate them into the Church by faith, baptism, confirmation and the holy Eucharist. The Holy Spirit is the presence of the redeeming Christ in the Church; as we say in the creed, he is the 'giver of life', the life of Christ. He is the power of God who comes to enable the whole people of God to live Christian lives. He is present in the word of God that is proclaimed in the Church and by the Church. He is present in the reconciling mission of the Church of which one (important) manifestation is the sacrament of penance or reconciliation.

Much of this is concentrated in the brief gospel of today. On the first day of the week, the day of the resurrection, Jesus comes into the room where the disciples were and greets them with the words, 'Peace be to you', *Shalom*. This was not just a conventional greeting. Before his passion, he had said, 'Peace I bequeath you, my own peace I give you, a peace that the world cannot give, this is my gift to you'. (Jn14: 27). It was the peace he would make by 'his death on the cross' when he would reconcile the whole world to his Father (Col 1:20). As it were to underline the meaning of his greeting he showed them his hands and his side, still bearing the scars of the crucifixion. They, as we are, were ransomed, reconciled 'at a great price', the shedding of his blood until death.

That is what lay at the heart of the mission to which he was now appointing them. As the Father had sent him to proclaim the saving word of the gospel, and to lay down his life for the reconciliation of the world, now he was sending his disciples to continue that mission. As the Spirit of God was active in the creation of the world, so he was to be active in redeeming all who would come to him by faith and made a new creation, the people of God. So he breathes on them giving them the Holy Spirit, the 'giver of life'. They are now made new and, filled with the Holy Spirit, they would be able to go out and proclaim the good news to every creature (Matt 28: 18-20; Lk 24:47).

Like Jesus himself they were to call the people to repentance, as St Peter did in his first sermon on Pentecost Sunday. 'You must repent', he said, they must turn to God with all the strength of mind and heart, they must let the word of God penetrate their inmost being, and they must be baptised 'in the name of Jesus Christ' for the forgiveness of their sins. Then too they will receive the Holy Spirit that Jesus had promised (Acts 2:38). So those words, 'Whose sins you forgive...' include the good news of salvation as well as reconciliation and forgiveness through baptism and the reception of the Holy Spirit who comes to them in word and sacrament.

But there is an element of judgement in the words. 'Whose sins you retain...'; the disciples could 'retain' sins, withhold forgiveness from people like Ananias and Sapphira who 'had lied to God', as Peter did; and as he also did with Simon the Magician who tried to buy the gift of the Spirit. 'Repent of this wickedness of yours' Peter said to him, 'and pray to the Lord. You may still be forgiven' (Acts 5:1-11: 8:18-24).

The Pentecost event was the fulfilment of all that Jesus had promised. In spectacular fashion the Holy Spirit came down on the assembly, probably including the hundred and twenty people who were all together with the apostles and 'Mary, the mother of Jesus...and 'several women' who had met in the room a day or two before

(Acts 1:14). As in the beginning the Spirit of the Lord had filled the whole world, so now the Holy Spirit filled the whole infant Church. The Spirit permeated and activated the whole Church so that, in the terms of the Constitution on the Church of Vatican II, it became the 'instrument' and 'sacrament' of Jesus Christ and of his saving word and work. In this the disciples, now called apostles, men sent, would have a leading role. They, with others, proclaimed the good news, they gathered the people together to teach them, to break the bread of the Eucharist and to join in prayer with them (Acts 2: 42). It was in these ways that the Holy Spirit was communicated to the many who approached the community of Christ.

But, as the second reading shows, the gifts of the Spirit are various and are not the perquisite of the clergy. The gifts work 'in all sorts of different ways in different people' and the Spirit is given to each one 'for a good purpose'. And those good purposes from apostleship to administration are described in several places in the New Testament. They are the now well known *charismata* or charisms which must not be 'quenched' by the clergy but must be discerned and, when genuine, must be fostered. But it is sometimes forgotten that not all apparent charisms are of the Holy Spirit. As St Paul emphasised, they are all given for the 'up-building of the Church'. That is the test. If they forward the mission of the Church, they are genuine. If they lead to the division of the 'one body', they are not.

The vision of the Church suggested by the scriptures today is that of the Spirit-filled body which is the 'sacrament' of Christ. It proclaims his word, by its life it manifests his presence in the world and by its sacraments it makes him present as Redeemer and Saviour. All who will listen to the word and accept the sacraments of salvation receive the Spirit who lives and works in the depths of the Church and in every human soul if they will have it so. This is the essential work of the Church and Pentecost reminds us forcefully that the Church is more than, much more than, a visible institution, indispensable as that may be; and when the institution bears down heavily upon us, it is as well to remember that it is the vehicle of the Holy Spirit who communicates the Christ-life to us, enabling us to live the life to which we have been called. If the visible Church is and always will be imperfect, if, as Vatican II said, it is *semper reformanda,* always needing to reform itself, it never ceases to be that holy thing, the sacrament of Christ and the instrument of the Holy Spirit who imparts to us God's saving love.

J. D. Crichton

THE MOST HOLY TRINITY

Exodus 34:4-6, 8-9; psalm Daniel 3: 52-56
2 Corinthians 13:11-13; John 3:16-18

You'll Never Walk Alone

T ODAY'S feast is in the section of the lectionary which is headed, 'Feasts of Our Lord'. We might find that surprising at first. However, the more we think about it, the more appropriate we see that heading to be. We do not really know Jesus except in relation to the Father and the Spirit. Hence, Holy Trinity really is a feast of Our Lord since it is the feast of who Jesus is.

This ties in with the way we think about who we are ourselves. For instance, our own birth or baptism certificate says who we are by giving information about our parents. When we introduce someone, we often say: 'This is John's sister', or 'Mary's husband', or 'a friend of my mother's.'

Our relationships are an essential part of ourselves. We are not isolated individuals. We are inter-dependent persons. 'An awesome truth' is how the U.S. woman theologian, Beverley Harrison, describes the way we depend on each other. She puts it even more forcefully: '...we have the power through acts of love or lovelessness literally to create one another.' That means that we depend on each other so much, we even have the 'power to thwart life and to maim each other'. But we also have the power to love each other. She describes love as 'the power to act-each-other-into-well-being'.

If we human beings are so profoundly interdependent on each other as persons, we should not be surprised to hear Jesus speaking of a mysterious interdependence of Father, Son and Spirit within the very being of God. After all, we humans are made in the image of God. That is why it could even be said that today's feast is our feast too. As the Vatican Council reminds us, in revealing God to us Jesus has revealed our own selves to us.

There is something richly human – and divine – about the experience of togetherness. A few years ago many people were offended by the Liverpool fans at the Cup Final singing 'You'll never walk alone' during the National Anthem.

Maybe my red bias shows through but I found that profoundly symbolic rather than shocking. At the time our country was being deeply divided by government policies and the increasing numbers of the unemployed in cities like Liverpool were bearing the brunt of this. The gospel of individualism was being preached in our nation. It was even suggested that there was no such thing as society.

For me the singing of 'You'll never walk alone' by the Liverpool fans was their symbolic way of saying: 'If your idea of society is a nation of individuals, count us out. We will only recognise our nation, if our nation is prepared to recognise our togetherness with the rest of the country.' Through this symbolic gesture they were saying that the plight of the unemployed in Liverpool and cities like it is the concern and responsibility of the whole nation.

But the National Anthem is a hymn! Maybe so. But perhaps 'You'll never walk alone' could be seen as a kind of Trinitarian hymn. It celebrates togetherness and surely the Trinity is the source of all togetherness in heaven and on earth.

Trinity Sunday might seem to direct our attention towards God. But God quickly re-directs our attention back to our world. Today's gospel tells us that he loved this world so much that he gave us his only son. Just as the Lord passed before Moses in the first reading, so Jesus has passed before us. In his passing through our midst he has translated into the language of human living and relating what it means to be 'a God of tenderness and compassion, slow to anger, rich in kindness and faithfulness'.

This is the God in whose image we are created. Our mission is to continue this on-going creation by trying to put the imprint of this image on all the personal and structural relationships of inter-dependence in our world. To claim there is no such thing as society is to fail to recognise that human persons are essentially social beings since we are made in the image of the Trinitarian God.

Kevin T. Kelly

CORPUS CHRISTI

Deuteronomy 8:2-3, 14-16; psalm 147
1 Corinthians 10:16-17; John 6:51-58

A Community of Memory

I N AN AGE of unbridled individualism there is a constant danger of large numbers of people losing contact with their communal roots and traditions. If it is assumed that the isolated individual is self-sufficient and independent of any social bonds, then the place of the community and its traditions are put in question. This isolated individualism is damaging to the way we think about social and religious traditions, and is fundamentally flawed.

Christian initiation is not only about the individual's decision to believe in Christ but about his gradual acceptance in faith of the practices, values and beliefs of Christ's community. The Church is a community of memory, faithful to its past and committed to retelling the story of Christ and his people. It retells the story of the Lord in the Eucharistic memorial by proclaiming his word and celebrating the sacrament. As Christians assemble to celebrate the Eucharist in memory of the Lord Jesus, it would be wrong to see them as solitary diners at a public restaurant. They assemble in response to the call of the Lord Jesus to do this in memory of him. They come not as individuals but as members of the one body of Christ, the Church. The assembled Church is not a sociological group of people but is rather the Body of Christ, mysteriously bound together in Christ. Thus when the Church celebrates the feast of Corpus Christi it is celebrating at once the feast of the Church itself as the Body of Christ, and the Eucharist as the Body of Christ. This is why the Eucharist is called the 'sacrament of the Church': since in the celebration and reception of the Body of Christ the Church becomes that Body.

By commanding his Church to do this in memory of him, Jesus is not telling it to recall what he did on the cross and in his resurrection, as one might recall the memory of a friend or relative's death. For the Hebrew people, as for Christ, the word 'memorial' (*anamnesis*) when applied to sacred meals like the passover meant the actual and effective making-present of God's powerful works. What then is made present and effective in the Eucharistic celebration of Corpus Christi?

First, in the celebration of the Eucharist the Christian community remembers and makes present the stories of how God was and is active in his Word. In the reading from Deuteronomy the community is called to remember how the Lord led his people in the wilderness, how he

73

humbled them for their infidelity, and how he gave them manna to eat. Moses called the community of his time to remember these things lest it forget the wonderful works of the Lord. The christian community, in the context of the Eucharist, recalls these words of the past and now accept in faith their present power. The community of memory recalls the past and retells its story in order to make present the powerful and transforming words of God. The Church is called by the Word and constituted by it; it is subject to it and sustained by it.

Secondly, in the celebration of the Eucharist the christian community remembers how Christ became present in the blessing of the bread and the wine, and how his presence makes the community one Body, one Spirit in him (Eucharistic Prayer III). It is in the blessing of the cup and the bread that Christ, through the power of the Spirit, transforms the bread and wine into his own body and blood and, in Holy Communion, draws his community into a deeper communion of love with himself and with each other in him. St Paul in the second reading sees the Church as a communion of love bound together in Christ. For him the Church becomes a single Body in Christ through the prayer of blessing addressed to the Father in faith.

Thirdly, in the celebration of the Eucharist the Christian community remembers and retells the story of how Christ's once-and-for-all sacrifice on the cross becomes present in the Thanksgiving Prayer over the bread and wine. The ARCIC ecumenical statement on the Eucharist (1971) affirmed that in the Eucharistic Prayer the Church continues to make a perpetual memorial of Christ's once-and-for-all sacrifice, and that 'the benefits of his passion' are made present to his community. In the extremely sacrificial language of St John's gospel we are told that anyone who shares in the Eucharist does eat the flesh of the Son of Man and drink his blood. By using this strong language John does not mean in any sense a physical eating or drinking, since he is speaking in sacramental language. St Thomas emphasised that the sacrifice of Christ in the Eucharist is made sacramentally present. As the community gathers each time to remember the sacrifice of Christ on the cross, it is also called not only to remember, but to relive that sacrifice in their own everyday lives.

Patrick Crowley

THE TRANSFIGURATION (AUG 6)

Daniel 7: 9-10, 13-14; psalm 96
2 Peter 1:16-19 ; Matthew 17:1-9

Where was Mary?

I WONDER how many of us, when we hear the reading of the gospel accounts of the Transfiguration, have wished: 'If only I could have been there'. Not only to have seen the Lord, but to have seen him transfigured, to have heard him acknowledged by the Father as 'His Beloved Son in whom he was well pleased'. Yet I wonder what difference it would actually make in our lives if we had been there. Certainly the difference in the lives of Peter, James and John was not that great, when we consider their reactions at the time of the Passion of our Lord.

I cannot remember a time, since my earliest years, when I was not fascinated by, mystified by, the transfiguration. This immense miracle in the life of our Lord. Yet was it a miracle? I have now come to the conclusion that it was not. The miracle was, surely, that he did not live his life on earth in this transfigured state. Many, if not most, of us must have had to wait at airports for the arrival of one whom we love. We have looked around at the faces of others who are waiting. Strained faces, apprehensive faces, faces stressed until.... until the encounter with the person whom they have been waiting for and love. Then the faces become 'transfigured'. The word is surely justified.

But what has transformed those faces? Where has the tension gone? Where the apprehension? What has brought about the transfiguration of those faces? In a word it is love: a deep, transfiguration of love encountering love. Yes, that is what has brought about the change. Such a natural, yet supernatural, occurrence.

When Jesus prayed he encountered his Father in a profound, all consuming, love. That loving encounter brought about a transfiguration both of his countenance and his whole being. A truth shone forth; Jesus was the beloved of the Father; he was the fulfilment of the Law, signified by the presence of Moses; and the Prophets, signified by the presence of Elijah. The Love of God, the recognition of his Father, transfigured the countenance of Man.

Where, then, was Mary? Surely she, above all others, should have witnessed this transfiguration. She who had given birth to God incarnate must have had a right to see the flesh of the Word transfigured by the Love who is the Spirit that gave life to the Word.

Yet why should she have been there at the particular transfiguration mentioned in the gospel? Both the Son and the Mother would have been transfigured when they reached out to the Father of them both in prayer. The Mother would have seen the Son transfigured as surely as the Son would have seen the Mother transfigured. The power of 'Love-incarnate' was manifested in prayer.

If there be one thing lacking in the prayer of the individual Christian, or of the Church as a body for that matter, I believe it to be silence. Not silence in the sense of absence of noise, but rather that silence in which one can hear the Word of God in love and stillness. Neither the heights of love nor its depths can be encountered in noise or busyness. Yes, joyous acclamation does have its place in prayer, but so does silence. That is why the Lord used to go apart to pray, so that in stillness he could reach out to the Father and encounter him in silence. St John of the Cross wrote: 'God utters his Word in an eternity of silence; if we are to hear that word then we must listen to it in silence'. We do live in such a busy world, yet in the depths of our beings we must know a real need of... yes, stillness and silence.

Where did Mary ponder 'all these things'? In the stillness of her heart. This had to be. But even she, especially she, had to make space for that pondering; a pondering, a meditating, a prayer, that would reveal to her the reality of the Word of God and the loving purpose of the Father for the Son: even as she stood at the foot of the cross with a sword of sorrow piercing her own heart.

Contemplation is not for the contemplative monk or nun alone. It is for all who seek a deeper encounter with the Father, through the Son and in the Spirit in prayer. Each one of us would be transfigured, as would the Church itself, if we were to seek to become persons of true prayer, persons seeking to encounter our loving Father in prayer as did the Son.

Let us, then, seek to go aside with the Son in stillness, not only to see him transfigured but also so that we, too, might be transfigured by our loving encounter with the Father in prayer. Such prayer demands silence and stillness; such silence and stillness demands the sacrifice of time, yet what fruits that sacrifice will bear! Pray God the Father may acclaim each one of us in prayer as his beloved son or daughter in whom he is well pleased.

Anthony E. Sketch

THE TRIUMPH OF THE CROSS (SEPT 14)

Numbers 21:4-9; psalm 77
Philippians 2:6-11; John 3:13-17

The Son of Man Must Be Lifted Up

THE COMMENTATOR'S voice was getting more excited and shrill; the cheers were going up from the crowd; they were urging the competitors to give their best; it did not seem to matter which country they were running for: all seemed to share the joy and effort of those taking part. It must have felt like an age since they started to run, yet it was all over in a few moments. Then came the medal ceremony. The winner came forward to stand on the podium, and was joined by the second and third placed competitors. They were each in their proper places for the national anthems. The winner was higher than the rest. This is only one of the triumphs of our day, but we have also witnessed the captain of football or rugby teams being chaired off the pitch by grateful and excited fans. Triumph entails being lifted up.

The triumph of an athlete or a member of a team comes after lots of training and hard work, but it also the result of the person's own commitment and ability. The triumph or failure is examined to see what contributed to whatever happened. In the Old Testament the struggles of the people of God, as they continued their journey to the promised land were not always successful. The victories they gained could have been understood by them as military success, but their history was also wrapped up in the plan of God for his people. The defeats were considered as a reminder to them of the Covenant they had made and as a help to them to return to the ways of God. They were an indication that a spiritual change was needed. God could be against them, if they betrayed him by their behaviour. In the first reading God punishes the people, but we see that he also provides a remedy for them. In the defeats there is also an offer, a promise of salvation.

When they became a divided nation and the military triumphs were simply part of their history and heritage they began to look to a spiritual triumph over evil, which God would bring about for them. The suffering Servant would be triumphant over his sufferings and through them. Jesus is the fulfilment of these signs and through his sufferings triumphed over evil in the most perfect way completely. The cross for the Christian is means of our redemption, but from the time of our being at school we know that the cross was a means of execution. The people of the Graeco-Roman world saw the cross as a disgrace, a curse and most cruel punishment which was reserved for slaves. In many ways it must have emphasised to the Jews the fact that they were an occupied nation; it was a scandal to them since how could salvation come through a dead body, which was ritually unclean? They did not want the bodies to remain on the crosses; 'It was Preparation Day, and to prevent the bodies remaining on the cross during the sabbath – since that sabbath was a day of special solemnity – the Jews asked Pilate to have the legs broken and the bodies taken away.' The same horror of what the crucifixion or the suffering of Jesus would mean was experienced by those closest to him. They could accept his miracles, his healing, his teaching; they could acknowledge him as Messiah, but could not cope with him being rejected, scourged and crucified.

In today's Feast, we know there is a mystery about the cross, as we understand it. We believe that it was a necessary part of Jesus's mission to obey his Father, and to give praise and glory to him. In St John's gospel the cross is the glory. Christ is lifted up in the same way that he was raised from the dead. At the same time the cross is the means by which he gave his life for us and to us. Through the gospels we see it as the fulfilment of the prophets and psalms. The story of the two friends on the way to Emmaus indicates how the early disciples understood these last events of the life of Jesus. They no longer watered down what had happened. Jesus had said himself that we must take up our cross daily and follow him. So the cross becomes a sign to the Christian of what Jesus did for us, and an inspiration to him to lead the kind of life Jesus taught us. The disciples saw it as a privilege to share in the sufferings, so as to share in his glory. When the Son of Man is lifted up, he will draw all men to himself; Jesus is lifted up on the cross; he is raised to life, and taken up into heaven to sit at the right hand of the Father. All these thought are used in our everyday lives. We are raised up in triumph; as we saw earlier, we sometimes lift people up so that they can see or be seen. 'They will look on the one they have pierced'. A father may lift his child as a sign of love and protection. We sometimes say a person has lifted me up, meaning that they have encouraged me, made me feel better. Jesus brings all these thoughts together in himself. He is triumphant over evil; he shows the love and care of God the Father, lifting us up to share his life; he encourages us to look on him amid our difficulties, disappointments and scandals of our lives.

The triumph of the cross is that it enables us to look to Jesus in our suffering and weakness, and know he has been there too. We do not understand the suffering of the innocent, but are able to know something of the mystery of God who shares his life and love with us. The Son of Man must be lifted up, that is each of us, so that we come to be with God.

Anthony Shryane

ALL SOULS (NOV 2)

Isaiah 25: 6-9; psalm 22
Romans 5:5-11; John 6:37-40

The Family of the Church

I WAS SPEAKING to a friend the other day: he's a liturgist, but still a friend! He was telling me, as liturgists do, over a cup of coffee, that the earliest part of the funeral liturgy to be added to the mass and included in the *Funerals of Christians* when missals were being compiled was the section which was now part of our 'Final Commendation'. It was the section which reads; 'May the angels lead you to paradise, may the martyrs take you to the bosom of Abraham ...' It is a beautiful part of our Funeral Liturgy, and now it is often beautifully sung these days since the publication of the new *Order of Christian Funerals*. I was thinking about the sentiments which this refrain expressed and that they are most apposite for a day like today.

It is not by accident that today, the Commemoration of All the Faithful Departed, should follow on from our celebration of All Saints yesterday. It is a concrete expression that liturgy refects life, that the maxim *lex orandi, lex credendi* is as true as it is succinct. Our belief in the Communion of Saints is both firm and distinctive and it receives ample testimony in these days of prayer for those who have gone before us marked with the sign of faith, whether they have achieved their full union with God or not.

Our celebration of All Saints is magnificent, we recognise those countless generations who have faithfully handed our faith on by word and example and have achieved their destiny in so doing. Surely our questions about purgatory are not to deny those who have lived in like fashion, but await their eternal reward, a place in our prayer? Here is the crux, here is where the theologising tendency, which we have developed as a method of understanding our faith, can serve us less well than the more straightforward faith which has strengthened countless generations in their struggle to live the good life, to fight the good fight and achieve the crown of glory. The tendency to conceive of purgatory as an ante-room to hell rather than a final purification before union with God is certainly to be deplored, as is the notion that we can pin down the design of God in our puny catagories. Nonetheless, we would be foolish to assume that those who die are immediately fitted for the heavenly life by some mysterious act of God. The mysterious act of God is the sending of his son; the action of God is on earth and our response is to be lived – not to be prosponed till we have died.

Theology cannot oppose belief, our celebration is not morbid and garment-rending, it is a joyful realisation that despite the feebleness of our efforts the goodness and forgiveness of God are more magnanimous that we dare hope.

The Communion of Saints is one of the most magnificent and supportive models of the Church which can be conceived. It takes account both of the theology of the unity of our Church and of the legitimate human aspirations of the members of the Church on earth. The Church as family is an image both appealing and valuable in these days. Members of the family who have died are not forgotten; they are remembered with affection, and even their imperfections and foibles are remembered with certain fondness. They do not cease to be members of the family just because they are no longer present. With the Church the feeling can be even stronger since those who have gone before us achieve a more perfect form of what we all seek on earth, and we know that where they have gone we are sure to follow. That there should be a stage between humanity and sanctity seems to make perfect sense, even if it is simply a choir practice for the heavenly chorus. To commend our dead into the hands of the saints, martyrs and angels is an image which recognises the continuity of the communion of Church. The Church, gathered in the Funeral Liturgy, hands the dead person over to the Father, participates in the liturgy of heaven: one presence of God is left behind so that another presence can be achieved.

Today is our opportunity to pray for those who have gone before us, those whose sanctity is not necessarily a forgone conclusion. This is a state that probably includes most people and is the category which we ourselves will fall into when our turn comes. We have handed these over to the care of the Church in heaven at the time of their death, to illustrate our unity still we pray for them so that they in turn can care and intercede for us at the appropriate time. Having an awareness of the unity of the entire Church, not just the earthly one, is good for us. Today's commemoration can strengthen that belief and can lead us to an understanding of our own destiny. The family of God not only covers the earth, it rejoices in heaven and it fills the bits in between. Those of us who struggle take comfort this day in the possibilities beyond death.

Michael McMahon